the Old and New Testaments, and the question of how a text becomes sacred—as a result of the religious meanings it contains, or because of its acceptance by a community of believers.

Frank McConnell's lively introduction elucidates the book's themes, and provides a framework for the arguments of the essays which follow. Stimulating and original, *The Bible and the Narrative Tradition* is a welcome marriage of literary and biblical scholarship that pays respectful—and overdue—attention to the words that form the text of the "book of books."

About the Editor

Frank McConnell is Professor of English at the University of California, Santa Barbara. He is the author of *Storytelling and Mythmaking: Images from Film and Literature* (1979) and *The Science Fiction of H.G. Wells* (1981), also published by Oxford University Press.

The Bible and the Narrative Tradition

The Bible
and the Narrative
Tradition

Edited by
FRANK McCONNELL

New York   Oxford
OXFORD UNIVERSITY PRESS
1986

Oxford University Press

Oxford   New York   Toronto
Dehli   Bombay   Calcutta   Madras   Karachi
Petaling Jaya   Singapore   Hong Kong   Tokyo
Nairobi   Dar es Salaam   Cape Town
Melbourne   Auckland

and associated companies in
Beirut   Berlin   Ibadan   Nicosia

Published by Oxford University Press, Inc.,
200 Madison Avenue, New York, New York 10016

Library of Congress Cataloging-in-Publication Data
Main entry under title:
The Bible and the narrative tradition.
1. Bible as literature—Addresses, essays, lectures.
2. Bible—Criticism, interpretation, etc.—Addresses,
essays, lectures.   I. McConnell, Frank D., 1942–
BS535.B49   1946   809'.93522   85-29852
ISBN 0-19-503698-0

Printing (last digit):   9 8 7 6 5 4 3 2 1

Printed in the United States of America
on acid-free paper.

Acknowledgments

The core of this volume—the essays of Bloom, Frei, Kermode, and Robinson—were delivered at a conference on "The Bible and the Narrative Tradition" held at the University of California, Santa Barbara, in March 1983. Professors Robert Comstock, Robert Erickson, Michael O'Connell, Berger Pearson, and Everett Zimmerman were instrumental in the organization of the conference. Dean of the College of Arts and Sciences David Sprecher and Chancellor Robert Huttenback both lent their full support and encouragement to the project. It is a great pleasure to be able sincerely to acknowledge the help of so many valued fellow-laborers in the field, not only for the gift of their intelligence and counsel, but also for their apparently inexhaustible reserves of time. To them, this volume is dedicated.

Santa Barbara   F. M.
12 June 1985

Contents

The Bible and the Narrative Tradition

Introduction

FRANK McCONNELL

Early on in the *Mahabharata*, the great Hindu epic and arguably the greatest of all epics, the monk Utanka announces that "whatever is found in this story may be found somewhere else; but nothing found anywhere else will not be found in this story."

It is an astonishing claim—"I am the book of books"—and an unprecedented one. A book, for once, not only admits that it is a book, but announces itself to be the *book* of books, the compendium and summary of all the stories of mankind. Where else do we find such arrogance?

In the *Koran*, maybe. The second chapter or *sura* of the *Koran*— the first *sura* being merely a traditional, ritual prayer to Allah— begins, "This book is not to be doubted." Nowhere—not even in the *Mahabharata*—do we come across such an unmediated assertion by the text itself of its own holiness. Indeed, later on the *Koran* will promulgate the doctrine of the *Ijaz*: that is, the article of faith that the style of the *Koran* is inimitable, a doctrine that has exercised a permanent (and not altogether felicitous) influence upon Islamic poetry.

But the *Mahabharata* is an epic—a narrative poem with no serious claims to sacredness. And the *Koran* is a sacred text—a book to which narrative is merely an incidental concern. Both these strong works have their claims to a kind of cosmic encyclopedism. But the Indian epic makes that claim in terms of mythmaking, while the

3

Islamic gospel makes it in terms of divine revelation. A story may summarize all the stories of the world, in other words; and a prophetic utterance may utter the essence of all previous prophecies. But, we are bound to ask, could there be a book which did both at once—which could at least claim to be the essence of story *and* the kernel of prophecy?

Of course there is such a book, and its permanent presence in and pressure upon our civilization is the theme of the essays in this collection. The Bible spans the gap between narrative and prophecy (we will invent more complex terms for them later). It begins, *Bereshit*, "In the beginning," which may be the most wholly satisfactory opening any story can have; compare, for example, that opening favored by the world's best critics of storytelling, "Once upon a time." And from that absolutely narrative opening it moves, through the most complex of structures, toward the mighty and stunning assertion that is almost the last sentence of the book of Revelation: "If any man take away from the words of the book of this prophecy, God shall take away his part out of the book of life." The book has become an equivalent, in its sheer existence, to the salvation of the soul or of the people. This is a cultural phenomenon of the most cataclysmic order.

From folk-tale to structural self-consciousness, as a modern might say: the Book has the arrogance both of the *Mahabharata*, epic of epics, and of the *Koran*, a sacred text defining its own sacredness. That is the course, and the awesome range, of the book, the text, the immitigable *presence* we domesticate by calling "The Bible." No book has exercised a stronger influence upon the whole course of Western writing. No book has been subject to—or generated?—a wider variation of interpretations and perversions. And no book—this may be the central point of the essays collected here—has been less a book and more a living entity in the evolving consciousness of Western man.

The Bible: the name itself is a paradox. It comes from the Greek, *Biblia*, "little books," so that this most daunting of all texts is, really, an anthology. It is the one book we know which both *is* one, and is also the creation of a whole people. In 450 B.C.E., runs the legend, Ezra read aloud to the people of Israel the Torah—the first five books of the Hebrew Scriptures—establishing thereby the first official text of the Jews. But it was not until the first century C.E. that the great rabbis consolidated the Torah with the books of the Prophets and those variegated books called simply *kesuvim*, or "writings"; thus establishing the Hebrew Bible, the Tanak, as we now know it. Even as late as the second century C.E., the Rabbi Akiba had to argue mightily for the inclusion of his beloved *Song of Songs* in the canon, as one of the *kesuvim* along with Esther, Ecclesiastes, Psalms, Ruth, and so forth. Akiba won his fight—and, as Harold Bloom observes in his paper here, orthodox Judaism today is fundamentally the religion of Akiba. But these side-skirmishes of textual inclusion or exclusion, fascinating as they are, mask a deeper truth, a truth about the self-invention of the text itself. The late Samuel Sandmel, in his great book on *The Hebrew Scriptures*, puts it succinctly and powerfully. After the destruction of the Temple by the Romans, writes Sandmel, the older religion of animal sacrifice was supplanted by the veneration of the Book itself. "The Tanak," writes Sandmel, "became subtly changed from a prescription for how people should worship into almost an object of worship." The destruction of the cultic center meant the end of the old priesthood; but, by one of the miracles that sometimes convince us that human culture *is* human, the death of the cult was actually the birth of the rabbinical tradition, a vastly nobler thing.

There is probably no equivalent phenomenon among the other great religious traditions of the world. The Graf-Wellhausen hypothesis, formulated by two brilliant philologists in the nineteenth century, argues that the history of Judaism, as we can reconstruct it from the textual evidence, is a three-phase affair. It began as a primitive, desert religion, evolved into a moderately urban society dominated by the shamanic utterances of poets and prophets, and finally hardened into a priestly theocracy. The hypothesis still retains its brilliance, but—as Sandmel and others have pointed out— is wrong in one essential detail, and that detail is the fourth phase. What began as mythology grew into poetic and prophetic utterance, solidified into ritual, priestly observance—and *then*, through a disaster which was actually a kind of blessing, transfigured itself into an intellectual tradition which is, simply, the basis of all Western commentary on literature and the use of literature—including, by the way, the formation of the Graf-Wellhausen hypothesis.

Whether we read St. Augustine on the Fall of Man, Freud on the use of religion as social glue, or Jacques Derrida on the ontological primacy of writing over speaking, we are reading attempts to grapple with, to *use* literature as equipment for living: attempts which owe their urgency and passion to the urgency and passion they inherit from the great Rabbis and the early Fathers of the Church. This is a point made with great subtlety and conviction in Hans Frei's essay in this volume: that the intellectual future, as well as the exegetical past, of our culture is inextricably tied in with the tradition of scriptural-analytical thought. Of few, if any other books, may we say that to learn to read *this* Book is to learn to read.

But that is only part of the story of this volume, as it is only part of the story of the Bible and its influence upon Western storytelling. We have referred to the Tanak, which is the real name of what Christians (with unintentional prejudice) refer to as the Old Testament. But the Bible, in Western tradition, is not only one book— *The Great Code*, as Northrop Frye calls it in his recent study—it is one book frequently at odds with itself. I do not mean simply those ethical and narrative dissonances and contradictions which so disconcerted nineteenth-century scholars of an excessively literalistic bent. I mean the central fissure between the story of the people of Israel and the story of the radical preacher called Yeshua, or Joshua, or Jesus. I am aware, by the way, that in the very way I have articulated things, I have caused—not, I hope offense—but at least mild unease among some of my readers. That is not sheer perversity, but simply an attempt to indicate that Jesus *is* what St. Paul—that canniest of literary critics—called him: a scandal.

Frank Kermode observes, in his book *The Genesis of Secrecy*, that only once in the history of culture has a book had its entire meaning altered simply by renaming it: by renaming it, to be specific, the "Old" Testament.

Renaming, that is, *is* re-interpretation. This is a fact so common as to seem almost trivial, but nevertheless a crucial one for our understanding of the culture we create and the culture that creates *us*. To put the matter in its simplest terms: you can make a movie called *Star Wars*, and it will be a good or a bad film. But, then, what if you make a sequel? Are you continuing the story, or are you, in fact, reinterpreting the story by extending it?

Canon-formation, in other words, involves one of the deepest questions of cultural self-genesis. Are the great texts innately great, or is "greatness" simply the imposition and gift of societal consensus? Kermode's description of the exegetical feud between Childs and Barr, in this volume, is an intriguing and disturbing continuation of the inquiry he began in *The Genesis of Secrecy*: what *does* canonize a text—make a sacred text sacred?

As usual when I read Kermode, I was struck by the subtlety of the observation. And then I realized that Kermode was being more than subtle. He was being—as perhaps all good critics should be—both profound and threatening. Consider the enormity of the transformation involved in that single act of renaming. How can you say that the whole long, intense, tragic, tortured, glorious, epic, inarticulably difficult struggle of *that* people, that produced *that* book, should come down to the maunderings and meanderings of an itinerant faith-healer from the sticks? How *dare* you say it?

Well, we have. At least, for two millennia now, we have insisted that the Sacred Book of all Sacred Books is in fact composed of two unequal but equal halves, the one being the record of a people's discovery of the Law and the other being the record of an individual's discovery of himself as Son of God. How can epic collapse so irrecoverably into mere biography; or how can folk-sociology evolve so stunningly into existential self-discovery? A lot depends on which of those questions you ask; for the one you ask determines how you really think of the relationship between the two Testaments. And, of course, if you choose to be really civilized, you must learn to think both ways at once.

If Moses, as St. Augustine argued, was simply a "type" or "figure" of Jesus, the *real* leader of the people out of bondage, then the mighty tale of Genesis and Exodus is transformed, at a stroke, into allegory. Or, to put it the other way round, from the Jewish perspective: if the Gospels and the Pauline epistles insist so strenuously that Jesus fulfilled, to the last jot and tittle, the ambiguous sayings of the Prophets about the Messiah, then must he himself not be a convenient, cultic fabrication—rather like a back-formation in linguistics?

Most cultures would resolve this tension—and it *is* a tension—by simply treating the Scriptures as separate entities. The highly mysti-

cal *Tao Te Ching* makes, after all, numerous references to, and com-
mentaries upon, the very practical Confucian *Analects*—almost all of
them uncomplimentary. But no sane man would think of binding the
Analects and the *Tao Te Ching* together as a single, unified literary
utterance.

Perhaps this would have been the simpler thing to do with the
two parts of what we call the Bible. The Tanak itself is confused.
Ever since the discovery and discrimination of the famous four
sources of Torah—Yawhistic, Elohistic, Deuteronymic, and Priestly
—scholars of the Tanak have been unearthing more and more
variant sources in that part of the book alone. And, as James
Robinson demonstrates in his essay here, the same intricate, often
baffling process of redaction and conflation of sources seems to have
produced what we think of as the canon of Christian Scripture. The
Bible as a whole, old *and* new Testaments, can be described not so
much as the utterance of a single Author, or even series of Authors,
but rather as a formation like the accumulation of geological strata.
And given such complex histories of canon-formation for two texts
so subtly at odds one with the other, it would make elegant sense to
issue them, simply, as separate, if related, books.

But this is not what we have done. And by not doing it, we have
created the literature of the West.

"Intertextuality" is a phrase much bandied—or shuttlecocked—
among critics with a yen for the fashionable these days. Like most
such phrases it is not only phonetically ugly but, semantically,
virtually null. If it does have a meaning, though, it appears to refer
to the ways a given text refers to itself, within itself, as a text: or as
a "heterocosm," to use another fashionable term—that is, a verbal
universe that equals or rivals the "real" universe of our experience.
But is this not the Bible? I repeat myself: to learn to read *this* book is
to learn to read. And, at least for Western man, to learn to read is to
learn something about how to live: or so we trust.

The "intertextuality" of the Bible, then—if we must call it
that—may be taken as the paradigm for that "intertextuality"
which, though only recently named as such, has in fact determined
the course of Western storytelling. Does the "Old Testament"
simply anticipate the "New"? Or does the "New Testament"

simply parrot and attempt to fulfill the "Old"? Trivial sectarian quarrels aside, the answer of course is that neither assertion makes sense. It is precisely the *tension* of the text that makes it live—and that makes it a source of life for later, secular writing.

A comparison with the transmission of classical literature can be instructive here. We all know that the *Aeneid* of Virgil is an attempt—and a glorious one—to equal or surpass the Homeric epics. And we know that even a later book, like the *Argonautica* of Appolonius of Rhodes, is in its way an attempt to rescind, comment upon, perhaps even parody the pattern of classical epic established by Homer and Virgil.

But this is not "intertextuality"—at least, not in the sense in which the Bible gives it to us. Virgil may try to overcome Homer, and Appolonius may try to parody both. But in no case in classical writing do we find storytellers, from widely variant historical and cultural contexts, contributing mutually toward the creation of a single utterance which shall be the utterance of a whole world-view. We *may* speak of the classical world-view, in other words: but only by a process of agglomeration. But we *must* speak of the Judeo-Christian vision, because the text, in all its counterpoint, demands that we do so.

And yet, again, it is a unity founded upon a special kind of internal disunity. Consider the Islamic doctrine of the *Ijaz*, the inimitability of the style of the *Koran*. Any orthodox Muslim will tell you that to read the *Koran*, you must read it in Arabic. And with less rigidity, but equal earnestness, a Hindu will tell you the same about the *Upanishads*, or a Taoist about the *Tao Te Ching*. These are sacred texts whose sacrality resides, to a large extent, within the original text itself. But, from the Septuagint to the Vulgate to the King James to such contemporary versions as *Good News for Modern Man*, no book has been translated as variously or as frequently as the Bible. And the *translatability* of the book is special to its own central kind of sacredness. For it is a sacredness not only "intertextual"— that is, grounded in the story and the doctrine of the book. It is also—to coin a phrase nearly awkward enough to sound legimate— "extratextual," open-ended, infinitely and *necessarily* translatable both linguistically and culturally, just because its central core of meaning resides in the tension, rather than the intension, of its significance. We can say that it is *about*, among many other things, the creation of a sacred text.

This is really less complicated than it sounds. Without undue chauvinism, we may say that Western writing displays a tendency toward variation, growth, exfoliation unprecedented among most of the great literary traditions of the world. This is not to claim superiority; merely difference. Harold Bloom describes this process as the "Anxiety of Influence," that is, the compulsion of strong poets to equal and overcome the vision of their "precursors," or major influences. Thus—greatly to oversimplify Bloom's argument—Wordsworth struggles to "overcome" his strong precursor Milton, and Wallace Stevens struggles to "overcome" his strong precursor Walt Whitman. Obviously, this idea of the struggle with the precursor—or symbolic father—has deep connections with Freud's myth of the parental, Oedipal conflict: father and son fighting for possession of the maternal Muse, if you will. But it has an even closer homology with one of the truly uncanny moments of Genesis: Jacob's all-night wrestling match with the Nameless One from among the *elohim*, after which he wins his new name, Israel. Bloom discusses that incident in his essay here, as part of his fascination with the Yahwist, the earliest source of biblical narrative, and one of the few authors (Shakespeare being the only other) who seems absolutely without precursors in Bloom's sense of the word.

But is this not a version of canon-formation which is "extratextual" in our sense? The Yahwist's narrative is qualified by the later stories of the Elohist narrator, both of which are expanded upon and reinterpreted by the Deuteronymic and Priestly authors. To be sure, all ancient texts can be analyzed—like layers of geological strata—in terms of gradual accretions of meaning. But nowhere is the process so much an explicit part of the *meaning itself* of the text. If to learn to read the Bible is to learn to read, then we can also say that to read the Bible in terms of its self-evolution is to witness the birth of textuality itself.

The techincal term for what I have been calling "extratextuality" is *Midrash*. Roughly, it means the process whereby a later writer revises or even reverses details of an earlier tale to make it conform to the growth of ethical doctrine. Sandmel in *The Hebrew Scriptures*, for example, speculates that the figure of the patriarch Abraham, pious and noble, may be a midrashic back-formation, developed as a counterpoint and "precursor" to the earlier-invented and disconcertingly tricksterish Jacob. Or, applying the concept—which is really the concept of Western literature itself—to a "secular" text, we can say that *Paradise Lost* is Milton's seventeenth-century, Puritan midrash on the Yahwist text of the Fall, bringing that most primal of tales into synchronization with his own, baroque radical Puritan Christian interpretation of the facts of the case.

The recent discovery of the Gnostic Gospels—the Nag Hammadi Library—indicates that much the same process went on with the Christian half—or part—of the Bible. James Robinson, the guiding force behind the translation of the Gnostic Gospels, examines in his essay here the way in which the formation of the Christian scriptures is also a kind of "midrashic" process of composition. Particularly with reference to the Gospel of John, that most troublesome of all the Gospels, he explains with rare tact and clarity how an originally Gnostic, that is, heterodox, version of the life of Jesus is "naturalized" for inclusion in the canon, and then, paradoxically, by its very inclusion regains the Gnostic, or Gnostic-like, mysticism that its revision was originally meant to eschew.

The sacred canon—the Tanak and the Christian scriptures—is of course closed, and has been definitively closed since about the fourth century C.E. But, as Frank Kermode insists here, the "open" tradition of modern Western writing is actually a kind of derivation from, or analogy to, the idea of the sacred canon. Kermode examined this analogy in his previous book, *The Genesis of Secrecy*, and develops it here to invoke what amounts to a redefinition of the literary tradition in terms of a biblical-canonical model. The "Anxiety of Influence," in other words, might also be imagined as "the self-expansion of inheritance."

We are dealing, then, with two complementary—or opposed?—ideas of the nature of writing in the West, and of the relationship of that writing to what is, for us, the Text of texts. As Kermode puts things, is canon—the official establishment of a set of "authoritative" books—a curse or a blessing? It was Mark Twain who defined a "classic" as a book that everyone admired and nobody read. But that is not just a good punchline, it is an encapsulated history of biblical exegesis. What is the *meaning* of Scripture, and where does that meaning reside—in the text itself or in the acceptance of the text by the community of belief? If the Judeo-Christian Bible is "extratextual" in the sense I have tried to indicate, does this not mean that, somehow, the whole *idea* of the text dissipates? All of our writers in this volume confront, in their various ways, the uncomfortable contemporary conviction—exported mainly from France—that the "meaning" of literature may be simply the infinite reassertion of the structures of consciousness itself, that "meaning" itself may indeed be the central myth or self-delusion of our culture.

It is a seductive idea, for it is an absolutely unitary one: it explains everything, at a stroke. But does it not also impoverish the infinite variability of the canon—sacred *or* secular—as we have it? One is reminded of Isaac Bashevis Singer's parable of the last demon in Poland. Since people have ceased believing in them, the demon population has radically depleted; and the very last demon takes refuge in a single letter of the one remaining copy of the Talmud. It is an aleph.

This is not to claim that Singer's fable refutes the elegant phenomenology of Jacques Lacan, Jacques Derrida, or their cohorts. But there *is* some point, I believe, in insisting that our sacred texts be allowed to retain their sacredness, their demons hiding in the alephs. Otherwise, in Mark Twain's terms, we need not read the "classics" anymore, we need simply to acknowledge their primacy. And to acknowledge their primacy under those conditions is to lose it.

Of course, you will have noticed that I am using the term, "sacred text," in an increasingly loose sense. By "sacred text" do I now mean Genesis, the Gospel of Mark, or *The Divine Comedy*—or even, for that matter, *Finnegans Wake?*

Perhaps the most exciting and challenging idea to emerge from the essays collected here is the sheer problem of deciding what makes a text "sacred"—or, conversely, what "sacred" can possibly mean when applied to a written text. Both Schleiermacher and Coleridge, the two great architects of modern exegesis, insisted, in their different ways, that any text, if read in the right spirit, is religious. The text *finds you*, as Coleridge was fond of saying. Alice in Wonderland, that most intrepid of mental adventurers, frequently saves herself from spiralling into madness by repeating the most boring, tautological of propositions. Are these, then, "sacred texts"?

Is a sacred text, in other words, *anything* that gets you through the night? A comic book, a TV show, a postcard from a friend—a glass of gin? You see where we have come to. To examine "The Bible and the Narrative Tradition" is, ultimately, to examine the nature of Western identity itself. V. Piatagorsky, the regnant genius of the Tartu School of linguistics, has devoted much of his career to defining what it is that gives a text that peculiar, evanescent quality of sacredness.

And one of Piatagorsky's findings is echoed and elaborated here by Hans Frei. A sacred text, Frei insists, is sacred because a given community *believes* it to be sacred, and accepts and *declares* it as such. In other words, at a single brilliant and admirable stroke, Frei resolves the problem of textuality and canonicity by saying that the canon can *only* be established within a community of believers—in a Church, in other words.

Frei takes a highly, and articulately, conservative stance toward the relationship between "sacred" and "secular" writing. A minister himself, he opts for the primacy of private interpretation as the real "meaning" of Scripture, a creative interchange between text and reader. But the central point of his complex and brilliant essay is that it tries to make this whole book irrelevant. For if Frei is correct, then the only future possible for biblical exegesis is an irrevocable fissure between cultural acceptance and cultic acceptance of the "truth" or "meaning" of the Bible. The alternatives are, that is, belief in the literal meaning of the text *within* a community of faith, or analysis of the "outside" meaning of the text from the viewpoint of an abstract, disengaged cultural anthropology.

It is instructive to compare and contrast Frei's comments on the "innerness" of the biblical canon with Frank Kermode's attempt to interpret that "innerness" from the point of view of one *outside* the community of belief. They are antithetical propositions, and in the tension between them resides much of the energy of argument in all the essays collected here. *Can* there be a sacred text without a Church to accept it as such? That is the real question posed by all of our writers: Does the demon (who might also be an angel) really reside *in* the aleph, or do we have to convince ourselves that he is there?

This is the crucial quarrel of biblical exegesis, at least since Erasmus defended the Catholic, textually-centered interpretation of Scripture against Luther's orally-centered romanticism. *Where* is the text? In the letters on the page? In the mind of the reader? Or somewhere—but where?—in between? Students of contemporary literary criticism will recognize that, *mutatis mutandis*, this is also the crucial question asked by our most distinguished readers of the "secular" canon—for example, Wolfgang Iser in *The Act of Reading*, Roland Barthes in *S/Z*, or Jacques Derrida in *Writing and Difference*.

In the midst of all this complication, it is worthwhile to remember that Martin Buber, one of the great modern commentators on the Tanak, assumed that the fictionality of Scripture—its resonance as cult *and* culture—is, far from being a disadvantage, its real normative triumph:

"Scripture does not state its doctrine as doctrine," writes Buber, "but by telling a story, and without exceeding the limits set by the nature of a story. It uses the methods of story-telling to a degree, however, that world literature has not yet learned to use. . . . Hence, it remains for us latecomers to point out the significance of what has been hitherto overlooked, neglected, insufficiently valued."

Buber's comfort is absolute, in other words, with the tension between story and sacredness with which we began: or, if his comfort with that tension is not absolute, at least it is absolutely asserted by his prose. But our authors, in their various ways, are concerned with examining the stresses that Buber, not ignores, but heroically denies. I began by asserting that the Bible *is* both the story of stories and the Text of texts. But one way of reading the essays assembled here, in their various brilliancies and various counter-tensions, is as a lengthy and intricate examination of the question, How *can* a book be both those absolutes at once?

Inevitably, we are approaching the idea of Gnosticism. And all the essays here deal variously with the issue of a Gnostic as opposed to a conservative or legalistic approach to Scripture—and, by extension, of course to secular Scripture.

It may help clarify things, at the outset, if I admit that I do not know what Gnosticism really *is*: nor does anyone else, including practicing (practicing?) Gnostics. But, relying on the splendid historical/cultural research of scholars like Hans Jonas and Gershom Scholem, we can at least say that Gnosticism is the belief that the *real* meaning of a text or a world (the *gnosis*—the Greek word for knowledge) is always concealed behind or within the ostensive meaning of that text or world. To be a Gnostic, then, is to be— literally—"in the know" about the secret meaning of the text or the universe (and, of course, to a true Gnostic those are always equivalent terms).

Gnosticism has lately become a very fashionable term and concept among literary critics. And the discovery of the Christian Gnostic scriptures is, to be sure, one of the most important literary/ archeological discoveries of the last two centuries. The issue (or doctrine, or attitude) of a Gnostic reading of the text, in other words, spans, in its very complexity, the gap between the secular and the sacred.

But there is another attitude: not superior, but antithetical to the Gnostic stance toward writing, and I am happy to give it a name which has a kind of punning reference to the idea of the *gnosis*. *Nostos* is the Greek word meaning "return home" or "homecoming," the root of our word "nostalgia." It is the word traditionally applied to the moment in the *Odyssey* when Odysseus reestablishes his kingship of Ithaca and, implicitly, the order of the universe. Both *gnosis* and *nostos* are un-biblical terms. And if the former implies a journey of knowledge and enlightenment beyond the boundaries of the known or the articulable, the latter is its ideal complement in implying a journey home *past* the ineffable back to the certitude of the quotidian.

Herbert Schneidau, in his book *Sacred Discontent*, discusses and examines this tension in Scripture by arguing that the real point of the Hebrew Tanak is its anti-mythic stance: that is, the Tanak for Schneidau is ultimately defineable as an insistence upon the historicity, rather than upon the mythic circularity, of God's action in the world—more *nostos* than *gnosis*, in other words. And his essay here continues the argument of *Sacred Discontent*, while expanding and refining it. Schneidau is concerned with narrative *as* narrative—with the fundamental process of storytelling itself. Narrative transcends theology, insists Schneidau early on in his essay. And he eloquently demonstrates that, as Coleridge would have said, the Biblical texts are best understood *as* narrative, and narrative itself is best understood *as* a form—perhaps the inescapable form—of sacred utterance. Analytic and deconstructionist as he is, Schneidau nevertheless returns us to the world of myth. *Gnosis* and *nostos* are one, here, not because of their innate resonance, but because of the pristine, adverting mind of their critic and commentator.

Robert Alter, in his own numerous studies of biblical narrative, sophisticates Schneidau's argument by pointing out that the prose of the Bible *alternates* between the circularity of pure myth and the open-endedness of pure chronicle, never deciding fully which it is. But Schneidau and Alter, and all later commentators are preceded here by the first man to comment upon the entire range, Hebrew and Christian, of Scripture—and therefore, in his way, the first truly Western literary critic. I mean Saint Paul, who wrote even before the Gospels were produced, and who insisted in letter after letter that the Law and the Gospel—the *nostos* and the *gnosis*—were best understood not as antagonists but as a creative tension generating a new culture. Writing to the Corinthians, those proto-gnostics, Paul can sound very legalistic indeed: and writing to the Romans, he can sound very much like a Gnostic himself. In his subtlety and his understanding of the complexity of interpretation, perhaps he should be made the patron saint of literary critics.

I do not know which phase, *gnosis* or *nostos*, best describes the use Scripture has for us now, though I suspect they both do, particularly if taken together. In this volume, at least, both attitudes are presented, and presented brilliantly.

James Robinson, a scriptural scholar of authority, examines here ways in which the techniques of literary criticism might be applied meaningfully to biblical exegesis. Frank Kermode moves in the opposite direction and attempts to employ our knowledge of biblical canon-formation to the idea of the invention of a secular culture. Hans Frei questions—and questions brilliantly—the whole enterprise of Robinson and Kermode. Can we, he asks, really use the methods of philology and textual commentary as a method of dealing with what is fundamentally a literature of *belief*? And Harold Bloom, if he does not quite answer Frei's question, nevertheless provides an utterance about the power and uncanniness of the earliest scriptural author which is not so much an argument as it is a *demonstration* of what an adverting mind can make of the Text of texts. Donald Foster, in his fine essay on the Gospel of John, turns the insights of Robinson and Bloom to original and, I believe, portentous use for further biblical studies. John's gospel has always been the most curious of Christian scriptures—among other reasons, because of its edgy relation to Gnostic traditions. But by combining Robinson's perceptions of canon formation with Bloom's important idea of literary "belatedness," Foster manages a reading of that complex text which is both faithful to the best traditions of exegesis and an act of creative critical understanding. Foster, the youngest of the contributors to this volume, augurs strongly for the perennial energy of the methods explored here by his senior colleagues.

Too often, Jewish and Christian texts are regarded as propositional disputations, quasi-metaphysical arguments about what is or is not, cosmically speaking, the case. The essays collected here, like much other recent work, help disabuse us of this notion. Comte insisted that the evolution of human thought is from a mythic, through a metaphysical, into a scientific or "positivistic" state of reason. But our scholars and critics suggest that the "mythic" level of thinking—the realm of storytelling—is more central and more perennial than Comte's simple-minded scientism suggests. We perceive, and share, the human state of things by narrative much more than by objective discourse: not, that is, by arguing about what *is*, but by trading tales about what, in the time of origins, *happened*. A valuable collection like Willis Barnstone's recent anthology of Gnostic and acpocryphal texts, *The Other Bible*, indicates the degree to which the formative quarrels of our tradition are, not about heresy, but about midrash, about alternative *narratives* to the (sometimes shakily) canonized narrative we accept "as Gospel." Literary criticism and scriptural exegesis, in other words, are not so much to be wedded as to be reunited after a—surely rather long—trial separation. The essays gathered here are, or can be regarded as, a set of epithalamia to that happy remarriage.

Martin Buber, in an unforgettable phrase, described the myth-making of the Bible as a "legitimate stammering": a hopeless babbling, that is, that still in all its hopelessness tries to name the

Unnameable and, perhaps, praise the Unapproachable. The great liberal Protestant theologian, Reinhold Niebuhr, argues much the same position in *Beyond Tragedy* when he examines the stories of the two Testaments as images of the unimaginable truth. As storytellers we are, in Niebuhr's Pauline phrase, "deceivers, yet true." Whether or not Western writing since the opening of the common era has sustained that holy task is a matter for debate. But the essays collected here suggest that we have, for all our confusion, continued to stammer, and to do so legitimately. Or, to paraphrase the *Mahabharata*, nothing that we stammer will not be stammered elsewhere, but nothing stammered elsewhere will not be uttered among us.

From J to K, or
The Uncanniness of the Yahwist

HAROLD BLOOM

To my best knowledge, it was the Harvard historian of religion, George Foot Moore, who first called the religion of the rabbis of the second century C. E. "Normative Judaism." Let me simplify by centering on one of those rabbis, surely the grandest: normative Judaism is the religion of Akiba. That vigorous scholar, patriot, and martyr may be regarded as the standard by which any other Jewish religious figure must be judged. If your faith and *praxis* share enough with Akiba's, then you too are a representative of normative Judaism. If not, then probably not. There is a charming legend in which Moses attends Akiba's seminar, and goes away baffled by the sage's interpretation—of Moses! But the deepest implication of the legend, as I read it, is that Akiba's strong misreading of Moses was in no way weakened by the Mosaic bafflement.

The Great Original of the literary and oral traditions that merged into normative Judaism was the writer scholarly convention rather wonderfully chose to call "J." Since Kafka is the most legitimate descendant of one aspect of the antithetical J (Tolstoy and the early, pre-Coleridgean Wordsworth are the most authentic descendants of J's other side), I find it useful to adopt the formula "from J to K," to describe the uncanny or antithetical elements in J's narratives. The J who could have written *Hadji Murad* or *The Tale of Margaret* was the inevitable fountainhead of what eventually became normative Judaism. But this first, strongest, and still somehow most Jewish of all our writers also could have written "The Hunter Gracchus" or even "Josephine the Singer and the Mouse Folk." Indeed he wrote uncannier stories than Kafka lived to write. How those stories ever could have been acceptable or even comprehensible to the P authors or the Deuteronomist, to the Academy of Ezra or the Pharisees, let alone to Akiba and his colleagues, is a mystery that I have been trying to clarify by developing a critical concept I call "facticity," a kind of brute contingency by which an author's strength blinds and incarcerates a tradition of belated readership. But here I primarily want to describe the uncanniness of J's work, to break out of facticity, insofar as I am able to do so.

By "the uncanny" I intend to mean Freud's concept, since that appears to be the authentic modern version of what once was called the Sublime. Freud defines the "uncanny" as being "in reality nothing new or foreign, but something familiar and old-established in the mind that has been estranged only by the process of repression." Since I myself, as a critic, am obsessed with the Sublime or Freud's "uncanny," I realize that my reading of any Sublime work or fragment is always dependent on an estrangement, in which the repressed returns upon me to end that estrangement, but only momentarily. The uncanniness of the Yahwist exceeds that of all other writers, because in him both the estrangement and the return achieve maximum force.

Of course, J himself is considered to be a fiction, variously referred to by scholars as a school, a tradition, a document, and a hypothesis. Well, Homer is perhaps a fiction too, and these days the slaves of critical fashion do not weary of proclaiming the death of the author, or at least the reduction of every author to the status of a Nietzschean fiction. But J is pragmatically the author-of-authors, in that his authority and originality constitute a difference that has made a difference. The teller of the tales of Jacob and of Joseph, of Moses and the Exodus, is a writer more inescapable than Shakespeare, and more pervasive in our consciousness than Freud. J's only cultural rival would be an unlikely compound of Homer and Plato. Plato's contest with Homer seems to me to mark one of the largest differences between the ancient Greeks and the Hebrews. The agon for the mind of Athens found no equivalent in Jerusalem, and so the Yahwist still remains the mind of Jerusalem, everywhere that Jerusalem happens to be.

I do not believe that J was a fiction, and indeed J troubles me because his uncanniness calls into question my own conviction that every writer is belated, and so is always an inter-poet. J's freedom from belatedness rivals Shakespeare's, which is to say that J's originality is as intense as Shakespeare's. But J wrote twenty-five hundred years before Shakespeare, and that time span bewilders comparison. I am going to sketch J's possible circumstances and purposes, in order to hazard a description of J's tone, or of the uncanniness of his stance as a writer. Not much in my sketch will flout received scholarship, but necessarily I will have to go beyond the present state of biblical scholarship, since it cannot even decide precisely which texts are J's, or even revised by others from J. My attempt at transcending scholarship is simply a literary critic's final reliance upon her or his own sense of a text, or what I have called the necessity of misreading. No critic, whatever her or his moldiness *or* skepticism, can evade a Nietzschean will to power over a text, because interpretation is at last nothing else. The text, even if it was written that morning, and shown by its poet to the critic at high noon, is already lost in time, as lost as the Yahwist. Time says, "It was," and authentic criticism, as Nietzsche implied, is necessarily pervaded by a will for revenge against time's "it was." No interpreter can suspend the will to relational knowledge for more than an isolated moment, and since all narrative and all poetry are also interpretation, all writing manifests such a will.

Solomon the King, nowhere of course overtly mentioned by J, is the dominant contemporary force in the context of J's writing. I would go further, and as a pious Stevensian would say that Solomon is J's motive for metaphor. The reign of Solomon ended in the year 922 before the common era, and J quite possibly wrote either in Solomon's last years, or—more likely, I think—shortly thereafter. One can venture that Solomon was to J what Elizabeth was to Shakespeare, an idea of order, as crucial to J's Jerusalem as it was in Shakespeare's London. The imperial theme is J's countersong, though J's main burden is a heroic and agonistic past represented by David the King, while his implied judgment on the imperial present is at best skeptical, since he implies also an agonistic future. J's vision of agon centers his uncanny stance, accounting for his nearly unique mode of irony.

How much of J's actual text we have lost to the replacement tactics of redactors we cannot know, but biblical scholarship has not persuaded me that either the so-called Elohistic or the Priestly redactors provide fully coherent visions of their own, except perhaps for the Priestly first chapter of Genesis, which is so startling a contrast to J's account of how we all got started. But let me sketch the main contours of J's narrative, as we appear to have it. Yahweh begins his Creation in the first harsh Judean spring, before the first rain comes down. Water wells up from the earth, and Yahweh molds Adam out of the red clay, breathing into the earthling's nostrils a breath of the divine life. Then come the stories we think we know: Eve, the serpent, Cain and Abel, Seth, Noah and the Flood, the tower of Babel, and something utterly new with Abraham. From Abraham on, the main sequence again belongs to J: the Covenant, Ishmael, Yahweh at Mamre and on the road to Sodom, Lot, Isaac and the Akedah, Rebecca, Esau and Jacob, the tales of Jacob, Tamar, the story of Joseph and his brothers, and then the Mosaic account. Moses, so far as I can tell, meant much less to J than he did to the normative redactors, and so the J strand in Exodus and Numbers is even more laconic than J tended to be earlier.

In J's Exodus we find the oppression of the Jews, the birth of Moses, his escape to Midian, the burning bush and the instruction, the weird murderous attack by Yahweh upon Moses, the audiences with Pharaoh, the plagues, and the departure, flight, and crossing. Matters become sparser with Israel in the wilderness, at the Sinai covenant, and then with the dissensions and the battles in Numbers. J flares up finally on a grand scale in the serio-comic Balaam and Balak episode, but that is not the end of J's work, even as we have it. The Deuteronomist memorably incorporates J in his chapters 31 and 34, dealing with the death of Moses. I give here in sequence the opening and the close of what we hear J's Yahweh speaking aloud, to Adam and then to Moses. First, to Adam: "Of every tree in the garden you are free to eat; but as for the tree of knowledge of good and bad, you must not eat of it; for as soon as you eat of it, you shall die." And then to Moses: "This is the land of which I swore to

Abraham, Isaac, and Jacob, 'I will give it to your offspring.' I have let you see it with your own eyes, but you shall not cross there.'' Rhetorically, the two speeches share the same cruel pattern of power: "Here it is; it is yours and yet it is not yours." Akin to J's counterpointing of Yahweh's first and last speeches is his counter-parting of Yahweh's first and last actions: "Yahweh formed man from the dust of the earth," and "Yahweh buried him, Moses, in the valley in the land of Moab, near Beth-peor; and no one knows his burial place to this day." From Adam to Moses is from earth to earth; Yahweh molds us and he buries us, and both actions are done with his own hands. As it was with Adam and Moses, so it was with David and with Solomon, and with those who come and will come after Solomon. J is the harshest and most monitory of writers, and his Yahweh is an uncanny god, who takes away much of what he gives, and who is beyond any standard of measurement. And yet what I have said about J so far is not even part of the truth; isolated, all by itself, it is not true at all, for J is a writer who exalts man, and who has most peculiar relations with God. Gorky once said of Tolstoy that Tolstoy's relation to God reminded him of the Russian proverb, "Two bears in one den." J's relation to his uncanny Yahweh frequently reminds me of my favorite Yiddish apothegm: "Sleep faster, we need the pillows." J barely can keep up with Yahweh, though J's Jacob almost can, while J's Moses cannot keep up at all. Since what is most problematic about J's writing is Yahweh, I suggest we take a closer look at J's Yahweh than the entire normative and modern scholarly tradition has been willing or able to take. Homer and Dante, Shakespeare and Milton, hardly lacked audacity in representing what may be beyond representation, but J was both bolder and shrewder than any other writer at inventing speeches and actions for God Himself. Only J convinces us that he knows precisely how and when Yahweh speaks; Isaiah compares poorly to J in this, while the Milton of *Paradise Lost*, Book III, hardly rates even as an involuntary parodist of J.

I am moved to ask a question which the normative tradition—Judaic, Christian, and even secular—cannot ask: What is J's stance toward Yahweh? I can begin an answer by listing all that it is not: creating Yahweh, J's primary emotions do not include awe, fear, wonder, much surprise, or even love. J *sounds* rather matter-of-fact, but that is part of J's unique mode of irony. By turns, J's stance toward Yahweh is appreciative, wryly apprehensive, intensely inter-ested, and above all attentive and alert. Toward Yahweh, J is perhaps a touch wary; J is always *prepared to be surprised*. What J knows is that Yahweh is Sublime or "uncanny," incommensurate yet rather agonistic, curious and lively, humorous yet irascible, and all too capable of suddenly violent action. But J's Yahweh is rather *heimlich* also; he sensibly avoids walking about in the Near Eastern heat, preferring the cool of the evening, and he likes to sit under the terebinths at Mamre, devouring roast calf and curds. J would have laughed at his normative descendants—Christian, Jewish, secular, scholarly—who go on calling his representations of Yahweh "anthro-pomorphic," when they should be calling his representations of Jacob "theomorphic."

"The anthropomorphic" always has been a misleading concept, and probably was the largest single element affecting the long history of the redaction of J that evolved into normative Judaism. Most modern scholars, Jewish and Gentile alike, cannot seem to accept the fact that there was no Jewish theology before Philo. "Jewish theology," despite its long history from Philo to Franz Rosenzweig, is therefore an oxymoron, particularly when applied to biblical texts, and most particularly when applied to J. J's Yahweh is an uncanny personality, and not at all a concept. Yahweh sometimes *seems* to behave like us, but because Yahweh and his sculpted creature, Adam, are incommensurate, this remains a mere seeming. Sometimes, and always within limits, we behave like Yahweh, and not necessarily because we will to do so. There is a true sense in which John Calvin was as strong a reader of J as he more clearly was of Job, a sense displayed in the paradox of the Protestant Yahweh who entraps his believers by an impossible double injunction, which might be phrased: "Be like me, but don't you dare to be too like me!" In J, the paradox emerges only gradually and does not reach its climax until the theophany on Sinai. Until Sinai, J's Yahweh ad-dresses himself only to a handful, to his elite: Adam, Noah, Abra-ham, Jacob, Joseph, and, by profound implication, David. But at Sinai, we encounter the crisis of J's writing, as we will see.

What is theomorphic about Adam, Noah, Abraham, Jacob, Jo-seph? I think the question should be rephrased: What is Davidic about them? About Joseph, everything, and indeed J's Joseph I read as a fictive representation of David, rather in the way Virgil's divine child represents Augustus, except that J is working on a grand scale with Joseph, bringing to perfection what may have been an old mode of romance.

I have called Solomon J's motive for metaphor, but that calling resounds with Nietzsche's motive for all trope: the desire to be different, the desire to be elsewhere. For J, the difference, the elsewhere, is David. J's agonistic elitism, the struggle for the blessing, is represented by Abraham, above all by Jacob, and by Tamar also. But the bearer of the blessing is David, and I have ventured the surmise that J's Joseph is a portrait of David. Though this surmise is, I think, original, the centering of J's humanism upon the implied figure of David is not, of course, original with me. It is a fundamental postulate of the school of Gerhard von Rad, worked out in detail by theologians like Hans Walter Wolff and Walter Brueggemann. Still, a phrase like Wolff's "the Kerygma of the Yahwist" makes me rather uneasy, since J is no more a theologian than he is a priest or prophet. Freud, like St. Paul, has a message, but J, like Shakespeare, does not. J *is* literature and not "confession," which of course is not true of his redactors. They were on the road to Akiba, but J, always in excess of the normative, was no quester.

I find no traces of cult in J, and I am puzzled that so many read as kerygmatic Yahweh's words to Abram in Genesis 12:2: "So, then, all the families of the earth can gain a blessing in you." The blessing, in J, simply does not mean what it came to mean in his redactors and in the subsequent normative tradition. To gain a blessing, particularly through the blessing that becomes Abraham's, is in J to join oneself to that elitest agon which culminated in the figure of the agonistic hero, David. To be blessed means ultimately that one's name will not be scattered, and the remembered name will retain life into a time without boundaries. The blessing then is temporal, and not spatial, as it was in Homer and in the Greeks after him, who like his heroes struggled for the foremost place. And a temporal blessing, like the kingdom in Shakespeare, finds its problematic aspect in the vicissitudes of descendants.

Jacob is J's central man, whose fruition, deferred in the beloved Joseph, because given to Judah, has come just before J's time in the triumph of David. I think that Brueggemann is imaginatively accurate in his hypothesis that David represented, for J, a new kind of man, almost a new Adam, the man whom Yahweh (in 2 Sam. 7) had decided to trust. Doubtless we cannot exclude from our considerations the Messianic tradition that the normative, Jewish and Christian, were to draw out from those two great contemporary writers, J and the author of 2 Samuel. But J does not have any such Messianic consciousness about David. Quite the reverse: for him, we can surmise, David had been and was the elite *image*: not a harbinger of a greater vision to come, but a fully human being who already had exhausted the full range and vitality of man's possibilities. If, as Brueggemann speculates, J's tropes of exile (Gen. 3:24, 4:12, 11:8) represent the true images of the Solomonic present, then I would find J's prime Davidic trope in Jacob's return to Canaan, marked by the all-night, all-in wrestling match that concentrates Jacob's name forever as Israel. The Davidic glory then is felt most strongly in Jacob's theomorphic triumph, rendered so much the more poignant by his permanent crippling: "The sun rose upon him as he passed Penuel, limping on his hip."

If Jacob is Israel as the father, then David, through the trope of Joseph, is Jacob's or Israel's truest son. What then is Davidic about J's Jacob? I like the late E. A. Speiser's surmise that J personally knew his great contemporary, the writer who gave us, in 2 Samuel, the history of David and his immediate successors. J's Joseph reads to me like a lovingly ironic parody of the David of the court historian. What matters most about David, as that model narrative presents him, is not only his charismatic intensity, but the marvelous gratuity of Yahweh's *hesed*, his Election-love for this most heroic of his favorites. To no one in J's text does Yahweh speak so undialectically as he does through Nathan to David in II Samuel 7:12–16:

> When your days are done and you lie with your fathers, I will raise up your offspring after you, one of your own issue, and I will establish his kingship. He shall build a house for My name, and I will establish his royal throne forever. I will be a father to him, and he shall be a son to Me. When he does wrong, I will chastise him with the rod of men and the affliction of mortals; but I will never

withdraw My favor from him as I withdrew it from Saul, whom I
removed to make room for you. Your house and your kingship shall
ever be secure before you; your throne shall be established forever.

The blessing in J, as I have written elsewhere, is always agonistic,
and Jacob is J's supreme agonist. But J makes a single exception for
Joseph, and clearly with the reader's eye centered upon David. From
the womb on to the ford of the Jabbok, Jacob is an agonist, and until
that night encounter at Penuel by no means a heroic one. His agon,
as I've said, is for the temporal blessing that will prevail into a time
without boundaries; and so it never resembles the Homeric or the
Athenian contest for the foremost place, a kind of topological or
spatial blessing. In J, the struggle is for the uncanny gift of life, for
the breath of Yahweh that transforms *adamah* into Adam. True,
David struggles, and suffers, but J's Joseph serenely voyages through
all vicissitudes, as though J were intimating that David's agon had
been of a new kind, one in which the obligation was wholly and
voluntarily on Yahweh's side in the Covenant. Jacob the father
wrestles lifelong, and is permanently crippled by the climactic
match with a nameless one among the Elohim whom I interpret as
the baffled angel of death, who learns that Israel lives, and always
will survive. Joseph the son charms reality, even as David seems to
have charmed Yahweh.

But Jacob, I surmise, was J's signature, and while the portrait of
the Davidic Joseph manifests J's wistfulness, the representation of
Jacob may well be J's self-portrait as the great writer of Israel. My
earlier question would then become: What is Davidic about J
himself, not as a person perhaps, but certainly as an author? My first
observation here would have to be this apparent paradox: J is
anything but a religious writer, unlike all his revisionists and interpreters, and David is anything but a religious personality, despite
having become the paradigm for all Messianic speculation, both
Jewish and Christian. Again I am in the wake of von Rad and his
school, but with this crucial Bloomian swerve: J and David are not
religious, just as Freud, for all his avowedly antireligious polemic, is
finally nothing but religious. Freud's overdetermination of meaning—his emphasis upon primal repression or a flight from represen-

tation before, indeed, there was anything to represent—establishes Freud as normatively Jewish despite himself. Turn it and turn it, for everything is in it, the sage ben Bag Bag said of Torah, and Freud says the same of the psyche. If there is sense in everything, then everything that is going to happen has happened already, and so reality is already in the past and there never can be anything new. Freud's stance toward psychic history is the normative rabbinical stance toward Jewish history, and if Akiba is the paradigm for what it is to be religious, then the professedly scientist Freud is as religious as Akiba, if we are speaking of the Jewish religion. But J, like the court historian's David of 2 Samuel, is quite Jewish without being at all religious, in the belated normative sense. For the uncanny J, and for the path-breaking David, everything that matters most is perpetually new.

But this is true of J's Jacob also, as it is of Abraham, even Isaac, and certainly Tamar—all of whom live at the edge of life rushing onward, never in a static present but always in the dynamism of J's Yahweh, whose incessant temporality generates anxious expectations in nearly every fresh sentence of certain passages. This is again the Kafkan aspect of J, though it is offset by J's strong sense of human freedom, a sense surpassing its Homeric parallels. What becomes theodicy in J's revisionists down to Milton, is for J not at all a perplexity. Since J has no concept of Yahweh, but a sense of Yahweh's peculiar personality, the interventions of Yahweh in primal family history do not impinge upon his elite's individual freedom. So we have the memorable and grimly funny argument between Yahweh and Abraham as they walk together down the road to Sodom. Abraham wears Yahweh down until Yahweh quite properly begins to get exasperated. The shrewd courage and humanity of Abraham convince me that in the Akedah the redactors simply eliminated J's text almost completely. As I read the Hebrew, there is an extraordinary gap between the Elohistic language and the sublime invention of the story. J's Abraham would have argued far more tenaciously with Yahweh for his son's life than he did in defense of the inhabitants of the sinful cities of the plain, and here the revisionists may have defrauded us of J's uncanny greatness at its height.

But how much they *have* left us which the normative tradition has been incapable of assimilating! I think the best way of seeing this is to juxtapose with J the Pharasaic Book of Jubilees, oddly called also "the Little Genesis," though it is prolix and redundant in every tiresome way. Written about one hundred years before the common era, Jubilees is a normative travesty of Genesis, far more severely, say, than Chronicles is a normative reduction of 2 Samuel. But though he writes so boringly, what is wonderfully illuminating about the author of Jubilees is that he totally eradicates J's text. Had he set out deliberately to remove everything idiosyncratic about J's share in Torah, he could have done no more thorough a job. Gone altogether is J's creation story of Yahweh moding the red clay into Adam and then breathing life into his own image. Gone as well is Yahweh at Mamre, where only angels now appear to Abraham and Sarah, and there is no dispute on the road to Sodom. And the Satanic prince of angels, Mastema, instigates Yahweh's trial of Abraham in the Akedah. Jacob and Esau do not wrestle in the womb, and Abraham prefers Jacob, though even the author of Jubilees does not go so far as to deny Isaac's greater love for Esau. Gone, alas totally gone, is J's sublime invention of the night wrestling at Penuel. Joseph lacks all charm and mischief, necessarily, and the agony of Jacob, and the subsequent grandeur of the reunion, are vanished away. Most revealingly, the uncanniest moment in J, Yahweh's attempt to murder Moses en route to Egypt, becomes Mastema's act. And wholly absent is J's most enigmatic vision, the Sinai theophany, which is replaced by the safe removal of J's too-lively Yahweh back to a sedate dwelling in the high heavens.

J's originality was too radical to be absorbed, and yet abides even now as the originality of a Yahweh who will not dwindle down into the normative Godhead of the Jews, Christians, and Muslims. Because J cared more for personality than for morality, and cared not at all for cult, his legacy is a disturbing sense that, as Blake phrased it, forms of worship have been chosen from poetic tales. J was no theologian and yet not a maker of saga or epic, and again not a historian, and not even a storyteller as such. We have no description of J that will fit, just as we have no idea of God that will contain his irrepressible Yahweh. I want to test these observations by a careful account J's Sinai theophany, where his Yahweh is more problematic than scholarship has been willing to perceive.

Despite the truncation, indeed the possible mutilation of J's account of the Sinai theophany, more than enough remains to mark it as the crisis or crossing-point of his work. For the first time, his Yahweh is overwhelmingly self-contradictory, rather than dialectical, ironic, or even crafty. The moment of crisis turns upon Yahweh's confrontation with the Israelite host. Is he to allow himself to be seen by them? How direct is his self-representation to be? Mamre and the road to Sodom suddenly seem estranged, or as though they never were. It is not that here Yahweh is presented less anthropomorphically, but that J's Moses (let alone those he leads), is far less theomorphic or Davidic than J's Abraham and J's Jacob, and certainly less theomorphic or Davidic than J's Joseph. Confronting his agonistic and theomorphic elite, from Abraham to the implied presence of David, Yahweh is both canny and uncanny. But Moses is neither theomorphic nor agonistic. J's Sinai theophany marks the moment of the blessing's transition from the elite to the entire Israelite host, and in that transition a true anxiety of representation breaks forth in J's work for the first time.

I follow Martin Noth's lead, in the main, as to those passages in Exodus 19 and 24 that are clearly J's, though my ear accepts as likely certain moments he considers only probably or at least quite possible. Here are Exodus 19:9–15, 18, 20–25, literally rendered:

> Yahweh said to Moses: "I will come to you in a thick cloud, that the people may hear that I speak with you and that they may trust you forever afterwards." Moses then reported the people's words to Yahweh, and Yahweh said to Moses: "Go to the people and warn them to be continent today and tomorrow. Let them wash their clothes. Let them be prepared for the third day, for on the third day Yahweh will descend upon Mount Sinai, in the sight of all the people. You shall set limits for the people all around, saying: 'Beware of climbing the mountain or touching the border of it. Whoever touches the mountain shall be put to death: no hand shall touch him, but either he shall be stoned or shot; whether beast or man, he shall not live.' When there is a loud blast of the ram's horn, then they may ascend the mountain."

Moses came down from the mountain unto the people and warned
them to remain pure, and they washed their clothes. And Moses
said to the people: "Prepare for the third day; do not approach a
woman."

Yahweh will come at first in a thick cloud, that the people may
hear yet presumably not see him; nevertheless, on the third day he
will come down upon Sinai "in the sight of all people." Sinai will be
taboo, but is this only a taboo of touch? What about seeing Yahweh?
I suspect that an ellipsis, wholly characteristic of J's rhetorical
strength, then intervened, again characteristically filled in by the E
redactors as verses 16 and 17, and again as verse 19; but in verse 18
clearly we hear J's grand tone:

Now Mount Sinai was all in smoke, for the Lord had come down
upon it in fire; the smoke rose like the smoke of a kiln, and all the
people trembled violently.

Whether people or mountain tremble hardly matters in this great
trope of immanent power. Yahweh, as we know, is neither the fire
nor in the fire, for the ultimate trope is the *makom*: Yahweh is the
place of the world, but the world is not his place, and so Yahweh is
also the place of the fire, but the fire is not his place. And so J
touches the heights of his own Sublime, though himself troubled by
an anxiety of representation previously unknown to him, an anxiety
of touch and, for the first time, of sight:

Yahweh came down upon Mount Sinai, on the mountain top,
and Yahweh called Moses to the mountain top, and Moses went up.
Yahweh said to Moses: "Go down, warn the people not to break
through to gaze at Yahweh, lest many of them die. And the priests
who come near Yahweh must purify themselves, lest Yahweh break
forth against them." But Moses said to Yahweh: "The people
cannot come up to Mount Sinai, for You warned us when You said:
'Set limits about the mountain and render it holy.'" So Yahweh
said to Moses: "Go down and come back with Aaron, but do not
allow the priests or the people to break through to come up to
Yahweh, lest Yahweh break out against them." And Moses de-
scended to the people and spoke to them.

However much we have grown accustomed to J, he has not prepared us for this. Never before has Yahweh, bent upon Covenant, been a potential catastrophe as well as a potential blessing. But then, certainly the difference is in the movement from an elite to a whole people. If, as I suspect, the pragmatic covenant for J was the Davidic or humanistic or theomorphic covenant, then the most salient poetic meaning here was contemporary, whether Solomonic or just after. The true covenant, without anxiety or the problematic of representation, was agonistic: with Abraham, with Jacob, with Joseph, with David, but neither with Moses nor with Solomon, and so never with the mass of the people, whether at Sinai or at J's own moment of writing. J is as elitist as Shakespeare, or as Freud: none of the three was exactly a writer on the left. Yahweh himself, in J's vision, becomes dangerously confused in the anxious expectations of at once favoring and threatening the host of the people, rather than the individuals, that he has chosen. When Moses reminds Yahweh that Sinai is off limits anyway, Yahweh evidently is too preoccupied and too little taken with Moses even to listen, and merely repreats his warning that he may be uncontrollable, even by himself.

As our text now stands, the revisionists take over, and the Commandments are promulgated. I surmise that in J's original text the Commandments, however phrased, came *after* some fragments of J that we still have in what is now Exodus 24:

> Then Yahweh said to Moses: "Come up to Yahweh, with Aaron, Nadab, and Abihu, and seventy elders of Israel, and bow low but from afar. And only Moses shall come near Yahweh. The others shall not come near, and the people shall not come up with him at all.

> Then Moses and Aaron, Nadab and Abihu, and seventy elders of Israel went up, and they saw the God of Israel; under His feet there was the likeness of a pavement of sapphire, like the very sky for purity. Yet He did not raise His hand against the leaders of the Israelites; they beheld God, and they ate and drank.

This is again J at his uncanniest, the true Western Sublime, and so the truest challenge to a belated Longinian critic like myself. We are at Mamre again, in a sense, except that here the seventy-four who constitute an elite (of sorts) eat and drink, as did the Elohim and Yahweh at Mamre, while now Yahweh watches enigmatically, and (rather wonderfully) is watched. And again, J is proudly self-contradictory, or perhaps even dialectical, his irony being beyond my interpretive ken, whereas his Yahweh is so outrageously self-contradictory that I do not know where precisely to begin in reading the phase of this difference. But rather than entering that laby-rinth—of who may or may not see Yahweh, or how, or when—I choose instead to test the one marvelous visual detail aganst the Second Commandment. Alas, we evidently do not have J's phrasing here, but there is a strength in the diction that may reflect an origin in J:

> You shall not make for yourself a sculptured image, or any likeness
> of what is in the heavens above, or on the earth below, or in the
> waters under the earth.

Surely we are to remember J's Yahweh, who formed the *adam* from the dust of the *adamah*, and blew into his sculptured image's nostrils the breath of life. The *zelem* is forbidden to us, as our creation. But had it been forbidden to J, at least until now? And even now, does not J make for himself and so also for us, a likeness of what is in the heavens above? The seventy-four eaters and drinkers saw with their own eyes of God of Israel, and they saw another likeness also: "under His feet there was the likeness of a pavement of sapphire, like the very sky for purity." Why precisely *this* visual image, from this greatest of writers who gives us so very few visual images, as compared to images that are auditory, dy-namic, motor urgencies? I take it that J, and not the Hebrew lan-guage, inaugurated the extraordinary process of describing any object primarily by telling us not how it looked, but *how it was made*, wonderfully and fearfully made. But here J describes what is seen, not indeed Yahweh in whole or in part, but what we may call Yahweh's chosen stance.

Stance in writing is also tone, and the tone of this passage is crucial, but perhaps beyond our determination. Martin Buber, as an eloquent rhetorician, described it with great vividness but with rather too much interpretive confidence in his book, *Moses*. The seventy-four representatives of Israel are personalized by this theorist of dialogical personalism:

> They have presumably wandered through clinging, hanging mist before dawn; and at the very moment they reach their goal, the swaying darkness tears asunder (as I myself happened to witness once) and dissolves except for one cloud already transparent with the hue of the still unrisen sun. The sapphire proximity of the heavens overwhelms the aged shepherds of the Delta, who have never before tasted, who have never been given the slightest idea, of what is shown in the play of early light over the summits of the mountains. And this precisely is perceived by the representatives of the liberated tribes as that which lies under the feet of their enthroned *Malek*.

Always ingenious and here refreshingly naturalistic, Buber nevertheless neglects what he sometimes recognized: J's uncanniness. Buber's motive, as he says, is to combat two opposed yet equally reductive views of Biblical theophanies: that they are either supernatural miracles or else impressive fantasies. But had J wanted us to believe that the seventy-four elders of Israel saw only a natural radiance, he would have written rather differently. The commentary of Brevard Childs is very precise: "The text is remarkable for its bluntness: 'They saw the God of Israel.'" Childs adds that from the Septuagint on to Maimonides there is a consistent toning down of the statement's directness. Surely the directness is realized yet more acutely if we recall that this is Yahweh's only appearance in the Hebrew Bible where he *says* absolutely nothing. J's emphasis is clear: the seventy-four are on Sinai to eat and drink in Yahweh's presence, while they stare at him, and he presumably stares right back. But that confronts us with the one visual detail J provides: "under His feet there was the likeness of a pavement of sapphire, like the very sky for purity." J gives us a great trope, which all commentary down to the scholarly present weakly misreads by literalization. J, himself a strong misreader of tradition, demands strong misreadings, and so I venture one here. Let us forget all such notions as Yahweh standing so high up that he seems to stand on the sky, or the old fellows never having seen early light in the mountains before. J is elliptical always; that is crucial to his rhetorical stance. He is too wily to say what you would see, if you sat there in awe, eating and drinking while you saw Yahweh. Indeed, we must assume that Yahweh is sitting, but nothing whatsoever is said about a throne, and J after all is not Isaiah or Micaiah ben Imlah or Ezekiel or John Milton. As at Mamre, Yahweh sits upon the ground, and yet it as though the sky were beneath his feet. May not this drastic reversal of perspective represent a vertigo of vision on the part of the seventy-four? To see the God of Israel is to see as though the world had been turned upside down. And that indeed Yahweh *is* seen, *contra* Buber, we can know through J's monitory comment: "Yet He did not raise His hand against the leaders of the Israelites; they beheld God, and they ate and drank." The sublimity is balanced *not* by a Covenant meal, as all the scholars solemnly assert, but by a picnic on Sinai.

That this uncanny festivity contradicts Yahweh's earlier warnings is not J's confusion, nor something produced by his redactors, but is a dramatic confusion that J's Yahweh had to manifest if his blessing was to be extended from elite individuals to an entire people. Being incommensurate, Yahweh cannot be said to have thus touched his limits, but in the little more that J wrote, Yahweh is rather less lively than he had been. His heart, as J hints, was not with Moses, but with David, who was to come. J's heart, I venture as I close, was also not with Moses, nor even with Jospeh, as David's surrogate, and not really with Yahweh either. It was with Jacob at the Jabbok, obdurately confronting death in the shape of a time-obsessed nameless one from among the Elohim. Wrestling heroically to win the temporal blessing of a new name, Israel—that is uniquely J's own agon.

The "Literal Reading" of Biblical Narrative in the Christian Tradition: Does It Stretch or Will It Break?

HANS W. FREI

An outsider to the lively, cacophonous discussion among contemporary theorists of literature is bound to wonder whether the very term "narrative tradition" isn't one more among the hypostatized constants, like the "canon" of literature or the notion of "literariness," which some of the discussants want to consign to dissolution. As a Christian theologian rather than a literary or biblical scholar, I shall not try to position the Bible in relation to this putative tradition; instead, I will comment on what I perceive to be a wide, though of course not unanimous, traditional consensus among Christians in the West on the primacy of the literal reading of the Bible, on its connection with narrative, on its present status and future outlook.

Much of the essay will be taken up with "hermeneutics," the theory of the interpretation of texts and of the character of understanding going into that activity. The exposition will be complex because both the theory itself and the criticisms often mounted against it today are complex, not to say esoteric. But the reason for the exercise is as simple as the exercise itself is difficult: In the midst of a mounting crescendo of dissent from thematic readings of narratives, including scriptural stories, as normative guides for living and believing as well as reading, hermeneutical theory is the most prominent contemporary champion of the embattled tradition. So if one comes to the conclusion that the value of this sustained and subtle effort is in the end questionable, one had best go through the paces of arguing the negative case. In sum, I believe that the tradition of the *sensus literalis* is the closest one can come to a consensus reading of the Bible as the sacred text in the Christian church and that current hermeneutical theory defends a revised form of it; but I also believe that the defense is a failure, so that, in the words of the essay's title, the literal reading will break apart under its ministrations. One may well hope that the *sensus literalis*, a much more supple notion than one might at first suspect, has a future. If it does, there will be good reason to explain what it is about with a far more modest theory—more modest both in its claims about what counts as valid interpretation and in the scope of the material on which it may pertinently comment.

This essay is therefore a strictly second-order affair, commenting on theories pertinent to the past as well as present and future *conditions* for the literal reading as a religious enterprise; it is neither an exercise within that traditional enterprise, nor even an argument in behalf of its continued viability. That viability, if any, will follow excellently from the actual, fruitful use religious people continue to make of it in ways that enhance their own and other people's lives, without the obscurantist features so often and unhappily associated with it. And even if, as may be expected, there is a continuing decline of the felt pertinence of this way of reading among those who do not make a direct religious use of it, this in no way alters the case for its viability in principle to Christian people, no matter how distressing it is bound to be to them as an actual cultural fact.

The association of narrative with religion generally and Christianity in particular has always been close, although the self-consciously systematic use of the concept "narrative" in Christian theology is a modern invention. Reference to "the sacred story" or "sacred" or "salvation history" as a category to describe what was taken to be the dominant content of the Bible did not arise until the seventeenth century.

Most, if not all, religions contain tales of creation, loss, quest, and restoration which symbolize reality and allow the readers or listeners access to the common identifying patterns making up that symbolized world, and to the communal ways of inhabiting it. It is generally assumed that such tales are originally oral in character, with no particular author, and that they are perpetuated by a tradition of authoritative narrators or singers. These tellers adapt the content and pattern of a common story in their own individual ways usually under formulaic constraints imposed both by linguistic conventions and by the absence of all ironic distance between narrator, story, and audience. Tellers and listeners are part of the same symbolic and enacted world, so that the conditions for self-referencing authorial or listening perspectives are lacking.[1]

Not all oral epics can become candidates for the status of "sacred stories" within "sacred texts," especially if one accepts the speculative theory that the distinction between "profane" and "sacred" is universal as well as primitive,[2] so that "folktales" come to be distinguished from "myths," which are of the same narrative order but include sacred themes.[3] However, the easy and natural fusion of historical tradition, myth, and social custom in ancient folktales makes for the natural inclusion of some of them in sacred texts, once the transition from oral to literate culture takes place.

However one speculates, in this or other ways, about the origins of sacred stories—and speculation it remains—most literate cultures have them and include them in their sacred texts. Contact and conflict among religions within the same demographic area or cultural family typically result in a parasitic takeover in altered form of the elements of one such text by a later, or even a contemporaneous, religious group as part of its own scripture. So it was between Hinduism and Buddhism, between Hebrew and Christian Scripture, and between Hebrew and Christian Scripture and the Qur'an. Sacred stories are obvious targets for such scriptural transformation. The adherents of Jesus did not obliterate the story of John the Baptist, assigning him instead the role of forerunner and witness in the story of Jesus and thus a secure, if subordinate, place in the Christian New Testament.

I.   The Primacy of the Literal Sense
in Christian Interpretation

The most striking example of this kind of takeover in the history of Western culture is the inclusion of Jewish in Christian Scripture by means of "typology" or "figuration," so that not only "Old Testament" narrative but its legal texts and its prophetic as well as wisdom literature are taken to point beyond themselves to their "fulfillment" in the "New Testament." The Jewish texts are taken as "types" of the story of Jesus as their common "antitype," an appropriating procedure that begins in the New Testament, notably in the letters of Paul, the letter to the Hebrews, and the synoptic Gospels, and then becomes the common characteristic of the Christian tradition of scriptural interpretation until modern times.

Two features in this process are especially striking. First, in contrast to Hebrew Scripture and the Rabbinic tradition, in which cultic and moral regulations tend to be at once associated with and yet relatively autonomous from narrative biblical texts, Christian tradition tends to derive the meaning of such regulations—for example, the sacraments, the place of the "law" in Christian life, the love commandment—directly from (or refer them directly to) its sacred story, the life, teachings, death, and resurrection of Jesus the Messiah. This narrative thus has a unifying force and a prescriptive character in both the New Testament and the Christian community that, despite the importance of the Exodus accounts, neither narrative generally nor any specific narrative has in Jewish Scripture and the Jewish community.

Second, it was largely by reason of this centrality of the story of Jesus that the Christian interpretive tradition in the West gradually assigned clear primacy to the literal sense in the reading of Scripture, not to be contradicted by other legitimate senses—tropological, allegorical, and anagogical. In the ancient church, some of the parables of Jesus—for example, that of the Good Samaritan (Luke 10:25–37)—were interpreted allegorically as referring latently or spiritually to all sorts of types, and more especially to Jesus himself, but this could only be done because the story of Jesus itself was taken to have a literal or plain meaning: He was the Messiah, and the fourfold storied depiction in the gospels, especially of his passion and resurrection, was the enacted form of his identity as Messiah. Thus, by and large, except for the school of Origen in which the Old Testament received a kind of *independent* allegorical interpretation, allegory tended to be in the service of literal interpretation, with Jesus the center or focus of coherence for such reading. In that way, allegory remained legitimate up until the Reformation, even in its supposed rejection by the school of Antioch. Typological or figural interpretation, which was applied not only to the Old Testament but to the meaning of extrabiblical life and events, including one's own, stood in an unstable equilibrium between allegorical and literal interpretations. An event real in its own right and a meaning complex and meaningful in its own right are nonetheless understood to be incomplete, and thus "figures" of the event-and-or-meaning that fulfills them in the story of Jesus or in the universal story from creation to eschaton, of which it was the effectually shaping centerpiece.

The title of James Preus's important book on the history of Christian Old Testament interpretation, *From Shadow to Promise*,[4] points out a basic distinction between two kinds of allegorical and typological interpretations in Christian "Old Testament" reading. The "Old Testament" could be understood as "mere" letter or shadow, a "carnal" figure in the most derogatory sense, to which the "New Testament" stood in virtual contrast as the corresponding "spiritual" or genuine reality, and the all but direct contrary of its prefigured representation. There is often considerable similarity between orthodox Christian allegorical reading of the Old Testament and its hostile, negative interpretation on the part of Marcion, even though the orthodox, in contrast to Marcion, insisted on retaining the Old Testament as part of Scripture. However, other Christian exegetes thought they were honoring the Old Testament texts for their mysterious, many-sided, and spiritual profundity in reading them allegorically. For others yet, allegory and thus the "carnal" tales of the Old Testament were an educational means by which God accommodated himself to an early, crude, and temporary human condition—a theme that resurfaced during the Enlightenment era.

Whenever the Old Testament is seen as "letter" or "carnal shadow," spiritual and literal reading coincide, and figural and allegorical reading are one. "Spiritual reading" in this context is that of those who are in the first place privy to the truth directly rather than "under a veil," and who know, secondly, that the reality depicted is "heavenly," spiritual or religious, rather than earthly, empirical, material, or political. But since it is the story of Jesus taken literally that unveils this higher truth, the "literal" sense is the key to spiritual interpretation of the *New Testament*. In this as in some other respects, "letter" and "spirit" turn out to be mutually fit or reinforcing in much orthodox Christianity, despite the superficially contrary Pauline declaration (2 Cor. 3:6).

On the other hand, rather than as *shadow*, the Old Testament could be understood as *promise*, that is, as pointing to a state of affairs literally meant but only incompletely or not yet actualized at the time it was written, such as the prophecy in Jeremiah 31:31ff., "The days are coming when I shall make a New Covenant with the house of Israel and with the house of Judah: After those days, saith the Lord, I will put my law in their inward parts and write it in their hearts." Not only was this saying taken to indicate the fulfillment of an earlier by a later historical event in a chronological sequence, but earlier and later are at the same time related as trope to true meaning; tablets of stone are a preliminary, imperfect figure for their *telos*, tablets of flesh. Much Reformation and orthodox Protestant exegesis was governed by this outlook. Figure and fulfillment, or type and antitype, are related along a temporal as well as a literary or metaphorical axis.

Interpretive traditions of religious communities tend to reach a consensus on certain central texts. We have noted that the literal reading of the gospel stories was the crucial instance of this consensus in the early church. What is striking about this is that the "literal" reading in this fashion became the normative or "plain" reading of the texts. There is no a priori reason why the "plain" reading could not have been "spiritual" in contrast to "literal," and certainly the temptation was strong. The identification of the plain with the literal sense was not a logically necessary development, but it did begin with the early Christian community and was perhaps unique to Christianity. The creed, "rule of faith" or "rule of truth" which governed the Gospels' use in the church asserted the primacy of their literal sense. Moreover, it did this right from the beginning in the *ascriptive* even more than the *descriptive* mode. That "Jesus"—not someone else or nobody in particular—is the subject, the agent, and patient of these stories is said to be their crucial point, and the descriptions of events, sayings, personal qualities, and so forth, become literal by being firmly predicated of him. Not until the Protestant Reformation is the literal sense understood as authoritative—because perspicuous—in its own right, without authorization from the interpretive tradition.

The upshot of this ruled use of the New Testament stories was of course bound to entail the expropriative rules for the interpretation of Jewish Scripture which we have noted, and all three cases of the procedure—shadow and reality, prophecy and fulfillment, metaphorical type and literal antitype—came to present modern Christian biblical reading with two enormous problems. First, how is one to acknowledge the autonomy of the Jewish scriptural tradition without a collapse of Christian interpretation? Even if you brutalized it, you needed Jewish Scripture; for what is a fulfillment without antecedents that need to be fulfilled? Christians could neither do without Jewish Scripture nor accord it that autonomous status that a modern understanding of religions calls for. The second problem is a natural extension of the first, and it has been mentioned by commentators from Gotthold Ephraim Lessing to Frank Kermode, by some in an upbeat, by others in a deeply pessimistic mood: Suppose now that the literal sense of the New Testament only prefigures a still newer reading that displaces it in turn, developed by a new set of inside interpreters who transcend the now old (i.e., New Testament), exoteric, or carnal to reach a new spiritual sense which, because it refers to the truth in its real and not veiled form, is identical with the *true* literal sense. That new reading could be a new religion, with a new story ranged onto the old—who knows, perhaps the Unification Church. On the other hand, it could already be history, for example the Ottoman Turks carrying the Qur'an westward, except that their hermeneutical triumph stopped short at the gates of Vienna. The new reading could also be the product of a vision of a new humanity in which the previous difference between insiders and outsiders, esoteric and exoteric, or spiritual and carnal reading would disappear: All humanity would be the true new church, reading past Scriptures in the light of their eternal and universal transformation. As Lessing envisioned it: "It will surely come, the time of a new eternal gospel, which is promised us even in the primers of the New Covenant itself." We will all be insiders on that climactic day.[5]

On the other hand, such a new reading could involve the discovery that the only inside information we have is that, Lessing notwithstanding, we are all outsiders to the truth, and the only point at which literal and true spiritual senses coincide therefore is not—as Christians have claimed—in the Gospel narratives, nor in any later substitute, but in the shock of recognition that, the road to truth being barred, there must be an end to the literal sense. Rather than all humanity being insiders, we are all outsiders, and the only thing we know is that the truth is what we do not know.[6] The very notion of a true referent of the narrative texts of the New Testament—historical or ideal, accessible or not—and of the textual meaning as possible truth in that sense is an illusion. For Kermode it is a persistent and haunting, perhaps even inescapable, illusion, since readers of narrative texts are forever caught up in their dialectical alternation of divinatory disclosure and foreclosing secrecy. For Deconstructionists, by contrast, the discovery of the illusory character of linguistic meaning as truth is liberating, and with that liberation comes a way of reading a text which reverses the prior belief that texts open up a world, into the conviction that the world (or a world) must be seen as an indefinitely extended and open-ended, loosely interconnected, "intertextual" network, a kind of rhetorical *cosa nostra*.

II.   Hermeneutical Theory, Deconstruction, and the Literal Sense

This destruction of "normative" or "true" reading means an end, among other things, to the enterprise called "hermeneutics." Right from the beginning of that enterprise in the early nineteenth century, the notion of a unitary and systematic theory of understanding (contrasted to the older view of hermeneutics as a set of techinal and ad hoc rules for reading) had been anything but neutral with regard to the Bible as a source of profound meaningfulness and truth. All texts are "understood" in accordance with their "meaning," and "meaning" in turn is a systematic and dialectical partner or counterpart to "understanding," rather than a textual equivalent of a Kantian thing-in-itself. To include the Bible under this polar subject-object pattern for interpretation was no problem in the systematic hermeneutical tradition, for the Bible belonged in this view to a certain class of texts that illustrated the structure paradigmatically. Indeed, it was often taken to be *the* text above all others whose "meaning" raised "understanding" to its very limit at the edge of mystery, to its diacritical self-questioning level, and thereby brought about in a single "event" the full coincidence of disclosive textual force with the understanding self's ultimate interpretive and self-interpretive act.

The older tradition of hermeneutics had long since been transmogrified. In one of its shapes it ended up in this century as Anglo-American "New Criticism," denying all creative status to the second-order activity which was now called "criticism" rather than "interpretation," and banishing (usually, but not consistently) the notion of textual reference to a contextual world, together with intentional and affective fallacies. The literary text itself had an unchangeable, almost sacred, status conferred upon it and became a self-enclosed imagistic world, structured by such devices as paradox and irony, which the second-order commentator must, above all, leave as they are and not translate into some didactic "meaning" by way of prose paraphrase. For all its difference from hermeneutical theory, this outlook shares with it a belief in the possibility of valid, if not invariant, reading and (despite itself) a sense of a common, humanistic world shared by the "literary" work and the reader. However, it is hermeneutical theory that has been the most recent, vocal defender of that tradition. A brief summary of that position, within which biblical narrative becomes a "regional" instance of the universally valid pattern of interpretation, looks like this:

(1) All texts are "discourse," even if, being inscribed discourse, they gain freedom from the person of the author. (2) The obverse side of "discourse" is "understanding," from which "discourse" and its meaning never gain freedom: The basic condition of the possibility of understanding texts is the transcendentally grounded universal dialectic between understanding and the subject matter to be understood. In other words, though the status of the text is one of freedom from the author, and it is therefore possessed of its own

meaning—"utterance" meaning in contrast to "utterer's" meaning, in Paul Ricoeur's terms[7]—utterance meaning is inherently related to an appropriating understanding. "If all discourse is *actualized* as an event, all discourse is *understood* as meaning."[8] Understanding (or interpretation) is an internal event; it is nothing less than the centered self or transcendental ego in that particular and basic mode. The dialectic in which this event is operational is when the understanding stands "before" a text, so that the text is its equal or superior and not a replaceable phenomenon controlled by the ego's own interests or cultural location, such as historical inquiry into the social or psychological genesis of the text. (3) Language is, of course, indispensable to this discourse-and-consciousness process or event, but linguistic "sense," that is, the semiotic structures and semantic patterns of discourse, must also be related to its function as an expression of preconceptual consciousness or experience. (4) There is therefore a thrust within language and natural to it, both in utterance meaning and its appropriation, by means of which it transcends itself *qua* semiotic structure and semantic sense (beginning with the sentence) through such instruments as symbol and metaphor and "refers" to a real world. (5) But obviously it is actually *we*, the language users, who refer linguistically, so that the reality referent of language is at the same time a mode of human consciousness or of our "being-in-the-world." Language is the way of realizing or enacting self-presence in the presence of a world of meaning and truth, which is at the same time "distanced" from us having its own referential integrity. (6) By a natural extension, metaphor and symbol (i.e., "poetic" language) are taken to be the modes in which language (and experience) can express the creative thrust of the centered self toward an absolute limit and the "world" espied at that limit. In other words, there is a "split reference" in symbol and metaphor, to self-presence and its being-in-the-world, and—through one of its modes, the mode of limit experience and language—to the disclosed presence of the transcendent as the limit or self-transcending instance of the "secondary" world accessible through poetic language. The "objective" world of "descriptive discourse" is consigned to a decidedly peripheral and ambiguous status in the situation of "limit disclosure." Theoreticians in this tradition of phenomenological hermeneutics tend to be as critical of "outmoded" views of metaphor that stress a descriptive rather than a creative role for it as they are of those who reduce metaphor to a rhetorical or decorative function. The "limit" and "disclosure" situation in which transcendence and understanding come together is the class to which biblical writings belong, and to which the concept "revelation" is at least "homologous."[9] This view is strikingly reminiscent of the "doctrine of revelation" of liberal and neoorthodox religious apologists a generation ago, who held that "revelation" is a "spiritual event" rather than a historical or metaphysical propositional claim; it is, in fact, the hermeneutical equivalent of this outlook.

One should note three consequences of this outlook when it is applied to a literal reading of the Gospels. First, if the literal sense means that the story of Jesus is above all about a specific fictional or historical person by that name, and therefore about his identification through narrative descriptions which gain their force by being ascribed to him and no one else as the subject of those dispositions, words, actions, and sufferings, then the hermeneutical position we have described entails a view of him as ascriptive subject chiefly in the form of consciousness, that is, of his selfhood as "understanding." Obviously, this view of what it is to be a person is consistent with, if not indispensable to, the hermeneutical scheme of "meaning-and-understanding." Like anyone else, Jesus is here not in the first place the agent of his actions nor the enacted project(s) that constitute(s) him, nor the person to whom the actions of others happen; he is, rather, the verbal expressor of a certain preconceptual consciousness which he then, in a logically derivative or secondary sense, exhibits in action. For example, *that* Jesus was crucified is not a decisive part of his personal story, only that he was so consistent in his "mode-of-being-in-the-world" as to take the risk willingly. One would not want to deny the latter as part of the story, but it is surely a one-sided simplification of what it is to be a person in a world or a character in a plot. The personal world in the hermeneutical scheme is one in which the status of happenings is that of carnal shadows of the true "secondary" world of "meanings" " understood" in "disclosure."

On a technical and specifically hermeneutical level, what is wrong with this scheme is simply its claim to inclusiveness and adequacy for the interpretation of all texts depicting persons in a world, quite apart from doubts one may entertain about the claims to foundational, inclusive, and certain status of any hermeneutical framework for the interpretation of all narrative texts. The hostility to all interpretation of narratives, in which "descriptive discourse" is not "subverted" in favor of "creative metaphoric discourse" "referring" to (or "disclosing") a "secondary world," is a natural, perhaps even necessary, consequence of this hermeneutics produced by a phenomenology of consciousness. By and large, the Christian tradition of literal reading, even in the late, liberal and historical-critical states of "reconstructing" the "actual historical" Jesus "behind" the texts, has resisted this reduction of the subject of the narrative to consciousness (and consciousness as "event") rather than agent-in-occurrence, and of descriptive to metaphoric discourse in the presentation of the way in which this subject was significantly related to a world about him.

Second, it seems that *any* kind of literal ascription of "meaning" to a personal subject within the narrative world is highly tenuous, if not simply dissolved, under this hermeneutical governance. The clearly and irreducibly personal focus within this scheme is constituted not by the "meaning" of the narrative but by the interpreter—that is, the "understanding" to which "meaning" is related. What narratives present (whether or not "literally") is not in the first place ascriptive selves that are the subjects of their predicates, not even really the self-expressive, centered consciousness or transcendental ego, but the "mode-of-being-in-the-world" which these selves exemplify and which is "re-presented" by being "disclosed" to "understanding." In the words of David Tracy, a theologian whose New Testament hermeneutics is a close reading and precise regional application of Ricoeur's general hermeneutics:

> One may formulate the principal meaning referred to by the historically reconstructed re-presentative words, deeds, and destiny of Jesus the Christ as follows: the principal referent disclosed by this limit-language is the disclosure of a certain limit-mode-of-being-in-the-world; the disclosure of a new, and agapic, a self-sacrificing righteousness willing to risk living at that limit where one seems in the presence of the righteous, loving, gracious God re-presented in Jesus the Christ.[10]

Not that one can have any such "mode" without personal ascription either within the story or in appropriation (is that perhaps the point of the solecism, "the principal referent disclosed . . . is . . . the disclosure . . ."?), but the ascription in the story is simply a temporary personal thickening within the free-flowing stream of a general class of describable dispositional attitudes. "Jesus" in the statement quoted names a meaning, namely (the disclosure of) a generalizable set of attitudes (self-sacrificing righteousness, etc.), rather than these attitudes being referred to, held, or actuated, by "Jesus." What is being set forth here in technical language is a view of the Gospel narratives which is far closer to traditional allegorical than literal reading: Certain virtues or dispositions are hypostatized, that is, they are the significant referents of certain statements, but to maintain the narrative rather than didactic shape of these statements there has to be a personal embodiment, an "archetype" Kant called it, to exemplify them. But the archetype is identified by the virtues, not they by him through his self-enactment in significant temporal sequence. At best the link between meaning-reference and ascription to a personal subject within the story is tenuous in this view. At worst it is eliminated. The irreducibly personal element comes only in the "re-presented" "disclosure" situation, that is, in "understanding" appropriation of the text.

As with dispositional description and ascription, so with the "kerygmatic" verbal expression of consciousness "re-presented" by the Gospels. To "limit" *experience* there corresponds metaphoric "limit" *language*, and the two have the same "referent." Traditionally, "the Kingdom of God" in Jesus's preaching and Jesus himself have been understood to identify or "refer" to each other. By contrast, in hermeneutical theory one subsumes Jesus's preaching, especially the parables of the Kingdom of God, under a more general reference. In Ricoeur's terms, there is an "extravagance" in the denouement and the main characters that contrasts with the realism of the narrative and constitutes the parables' specific "religious" trait.[11] Religious language redescribes human experience: "The ultimate referent of the parables, proverbs, and eschatological sayings is not the Kingdom of God, but human reality in its wholeness. Religious language discloses the religious dimension of common human experience."[12]

Whether in the form of described dispositions, such as those exemplified by Jesus, or in the form of redescribed experience originally expressed in nondiscursive symbols or metaphorical discourse, such as Jesus's parables of the Kingdom of God, the narrative texts' meaning, that is, their referent, is a reality or world transcending the teller within the story, the character within the plot, and the descriptive dimension of the narrative language (in the case of the parables). "Human reality in its wholeness" will in one way or another be the subject matter instead each time, though perhaps a bit more obliquely and allegorically in the case of the narrated ascriptive subject called "Jesus," and more metaphorically and directly evocatively in the case of the parables and the experience they express.

Even Aristotle's *mimesis* has therefore to be understood as creative or magnifying rather than reduplicative imitation in narrative: It becomes "a kind of metaphor of reality."[13] Released from its moorings in or as descriptive world, historical or history-like fictional narrative, depicting and ascribing plot and character, refers actually to the general transcendental condition which constitutes the underlying possibility of such stories, namely, the "historicity" of humankind in general and of each self severally. And what is that? "We belong to history before telling stories or writing history." "Historicity" is finally neither reference to specific events, nor a pattern in specific stories; it is their ingredience in or unity with the logically prior general condition of self as consciousness within a diachronic frame, which stories—indispensable but logically subsequent—then bring to expression.[14] Once again, "meaning-as-reference" is not only not true but meaningless without its polar relation to "consciousness-as-understanding," but at this point (perhaps one of several), the polarity is actually transcended into the unity of the two. "Historicity" is the referential meaning *and* the consciousness or understanding of it. As personal, ascriptive subject "historicity" is at once (positively) particular and (transcendentally) general; it is at once irreducible (as understanding) and eminently transcendable (as universal, metaphorically subverted descriptive reference).

In sum, then, the view that the notion of being human is inseparable from that of being an agent becomes highly problematic in a general anthropology of consciousness and its hermeneutics; but the irreducibly *descriptive* as well as any irreducibly personal *ascriptive* character of literal reading is even more problematic in this hermeneutical setting. Yet one variant or another of this theory, more than any other, has been proposed as a general and foundational justification for a revised traditional reading of the narrative texts of the New Testament. Numerous warrants for doing so have been adduced by the theory's adherents: The applicability to these narratives of such concepts as revelation, uniqueness, and yet (simultaneously) generality of meaning; the significance of personal understanding and appropriation; the claim to normatively valid interpretation which transcends, without ignoring, the cultural setting of both texts and interpreters; and the claim to diachronic continuity between presently valid interpretation and a tradition of interpretation reaching back to the text itself, in particular the tradition of interpretation that assigns a distinctive status to Jesus in these stories.

Indeed, this last consideration has been particularly important to those Christian theologians who have adopted this general theory for regional hermeneutical application to the New Testament. They have been motivated by a desire on the one hand to claim the unsurpassability of the New Testament narratives' ascriptive reference to Jesus, so that they do not become exoteric or carnal shadows, in principle surpassable by a later and fuller spiritual "reference" or "disclosure," but on the other to deny that this unsurpassability involves the invidious distinction between insiders and outsiders to the truth.[15] So they try to maintain that Jesus is the irreducible ascriptive subject of the New Testament narratives, while at the same time they make general religious experience (or something like it) the "referent" of these stories.[16] It is an uneasy alliance of conflicting hermeneutical aims. The theory simply cannot bear the freight of all that its proponents want to load on to its shoulders. Whatever may be the case in its other regional exemplifications, when it is applied to the New Testament narrative texts the result is that the tradition of literal reading is not only stretched into a revised shape, it breaks down instead. It may well be an eminently worthy goal to have a theology that is at once Christian and liberal, but founding its reading of the New Testament on this general hermeneutical theory is not a good means for achieving that aim.

The third consequence of appealing to the general hermeneutical theory as a basis for a literal or revised reading of the New

Testament narratives is simply that, no matter how adequate or inadequate the theory turns out to be in actual exegetical application, the very possiblity of reading those narratives under its auspices has to stand or fall with the theory's own viability in the first place. It is well to be clear on what this does and does not involve. Paul Ricoeur, like many others but in a more sensitive and systematic way, has drawn attention to certain distinctions that one may summarize as pre-critical, critical, and post-critical stages in reading or, in his own terms, first and second naïveté (with "criticism" in between). A similar (though not identical) distinction is that between the "masters of suspicion" and a "hermeneutics of restoration" or "retrieval." Post-critical reading, reading with that second naïveté which is done in correspondence with a hermeneutics of restoration, is the kind of reading that might well wish to be of a "revised literal" sort. It distances the text from the author, from the original discourse's existential situation and from every other kind of reading that would go "behind" the text and "refer" it to any other world of meaning than its own, the world "in front of" the text. And yet, this kind of reading has been through the mill of critically transcending that (first) naïve literalism for which every statement on the printed page "means" either because it refers not only ostensively but also correctly, naming a true state of affairs each time, or else because it shapes part of a realm of discourse whose vocabulary one can finally only understand by repeating it and in that sense (if sense it is) taking it at "face value." If the general theory of hermeneutics is to stand, it must persuade us that its appeal to a second naïveté and to a hermeneutics of restoration constitutes a genuine option between reading with first naïveté on the one hand and on the other reading with that "suspicion" which regards the linguistic "world," which text and reader may share, as a mere ideological or psychological superstructure reducible to real or true infrastructures, which must be critically or scientifically adduced.

An indispensable part or assumption of the theory, especially in explaining the possibility of reading with second naïveté, is that there can be a coincidence, a "fusion of horizons," in H.-G. Gadamer's phrase, between the strange, distant, in a sense even timeless, world of the text detached from its temporal authorial origin, and the present reader who, though doubtless part of his world, is also the subject transcendental to it. This position is a strong revision of the "Romantic" hermeneutics of Schleiermacher, for whom "understanding" was a direct dialogue between the reader and the spirit of the author, present in the latter's language. "If," writes Paul Ricoeur,

> we preserve the language of Romanticist hermeneutics when it speaks of overcoming the distance, . . . of appropriating what was distant, other, foreign, it will be at the price of an important corrective. That which we make our own . . . is not a foreign experience, but the power of disclosing a world which constitutes the reference of the text.
>
> The link between disclosure and appropriation is, to my mind, the cornerstone of a hermeneutic which could claim both to overcome the shortcomings of historicism and to remain faithful to the original intention of Schleiermacher's hermeneutics. To understand an author better than he could understand himself is to display the power of disclosure implied in his discourse beyond the limited horizon of his own existential situation.[17]

The kind of language used to indicate the link between "disclosure" and "understanding" in this theory invariably has a strong component that appeals to the experience of "historicity" or time consciousness, and the dimension of the link is always that of the present poised between past and future. Appeals to synchronic links or to spatial metaphors are either secondary or diachronically intended in the language of this theory, so that (e.g.) "present" is the antonym of "past" rather than either the synonym of "near" or the antonym of "far." "Distance" and "distanciation" have a clearly diachronic ring in the theory's use of them. In cases such as the interpretation of the New Testament narratives, this temporal outlook is very clear indeed. Their "meaning," we have noted, is "represented" to the understanding. There is no proper understanding of texts from the past, "distanced" or released from their original moorings, except on the model (or, rather, more than the model) of a temporally present event, an event in or of contemporary consciousness.

Why this absolute centrality of the link between disclosure through text and the world to which it refers, and the temporally present event of understanding? No doubt there are many reasons, but surely one of the chief is simply a set of conceptual needs: One *needs* to have the text refer to or open up a (usually diachronic) world, if it is not merely to function as an instance of an internally connected general semiotic system or code in which the specific linguistic content or message ("parole" in contrast to "langue," in Saussure's famous formula) is no more than a trivial surface phenomenon. Furthermore, one *needs* to have the text open up a world independent of the text's cultural origins and every other reductive explanation, if we are going to have a hermeneutics in which understanding a text entails normative and valid exegetical interpretation, in a word a hermeneutics for "second naïveté." One *needs*, finally and foremost, to have a text both atemporally distanced from its moorings in a cultural and authorial or existential past and yet also re-entering the temporal dimension at the point of the present, if it is going to have the capacity to inform an understanding that is itself essentially characterized as present, in a word a hermeneutics of restoration. And yet this present re-entry of the text must not be a function or predicate of the presently understanding self—else it is illusory self-projection. "Disclosure" is a term satisfying these needs: The text is normative, in fact it transcends present understanding *ontologically*, but only in such a way that it is in principle *hermeneutically* focused toward the latter. Textual "disclosure" means that the language of the text "refers," but refers strictly in the mode of presentness. It also means that language, especially metaphoric language, refers creatively without creating what it refers to. "Disclosure" answers the need for and reality of a genuine convergence into coincidence of referential meaning and understanding.

The language of the text in opening up a world is simultaneously opened up by it. That simultaneity prevents language from turning either into simple descriptive, that is, falsely representational ("objectivist") language, or into being captured by purely "subjectivist" and self-projecting understanding. We *must* have "disclosure" if we are to have a hermeneutics that respects Heidegger's affirmation that language speaks because it indwells a world, instead of a hermeneutics that is a linguistic replica of the Cartesian error of separating out a self-contained, self-certain ego of "understandiing" from the understood world. In the case of our hermeneutical theory, the Cartesian error can be avoided only if the disclosure that fills this need of text and world "opening up" each other to present understanding is at least possibly true, in order to avoid the conclusion that understanding is simply the bedrock upon which it creates its own world in which it dwells and which it discloses to itself.

The world of the text's reference must be disclosed as a *possibly true* world. Meaning in disclosure has an ontological reference, and it is not clear whether the distinction between "possible" and "actual" truth is very sharp in "meaning as reference." In reference to general or possible truths, the matter is not significant, but only in individual instances, since "possible truth" is logically and ontologically dependent on the priority of "actual truth." In this respect as in others there is for the theory a real parallel to the claims of ostensive reference which, whether true or false in given instances, would make no sense except if there is an actual class of such items. Likewise, there must be ontological truth in the notion "textual reference to a world in disclosure" generally, if any particular case of it is to be possible and thus meaningful. I take this to be implied when Ricoeur writes: "The text speaks of a possible world and of a possible way of orienting oneself within it. The dimensions of this world are properly opened up by, disclosed by, the text. Disclosure is the equivalent for written language of ostensive reference for spoken language."[18]

Here, then, is the claim to a recovery of that view in which texts can in principle be normatively or validly interpreted because they refer to a truly possible world—a world Kermode declared to be either inaccessible throught the text or illusory in the first place, and one which Nietzsche and Derrida have taken, if anything, to be worse than illusory because it is no more than the fruit of a wishful misuse of texts. Neither a set of conceptual *needs* arising out of a certain understanding of language as a sign system, say such critics, nor the supply of a set of *answers* to them are necessarily persuasive because the two, needs and answers, cohere. One might well expect them to do so, because that is the way to meet the need intra-systematically; but that very fact might strengthen the suspicion that this is a case of systematic legerdemain, which is bound to produce a built-in verbal solution for every real or imagined conceptual problem. The system is an all-encompassing structure in which "meaning-and-understanding'' have set the foundational, inescapable terms, and "disclosure" is the equally inescapable, universal link between them.

"Disclosure" as an "event" in "understanding" is something of which many people testify they are ignorant. They say that this is not *their* model for what it is to understand, at least not one that holds pervasively. The advocates of the theory tend simply to respond that whether or not they understand that understanding is of this sort, that is in fact the case; and then they reiterate the theory in the hope that the reiteration will evoke the experiential correlate as an echo. And there the impassse remains.

Deconstruction, a deliberate subversion of this theory as of many others, is not identical with the strictly anti-hermeneutical procedure of "suspicion," with which hermeneutical theorists have understood themselves to be in sharp contention. The "masters of suspicion" simply dismiss the immanent, directly fitting *interpretive* structure which supports a textual reading of "second naïveté," supplanting it instead with an independent and wholly external *explanatory* frame. However, unlike Structuralist, Freudian, Marxist, and other theories of suspicion, Deconstruction is not *tout court* "a modern inheritor of [the] belief that reality, and our experience of it, are discontinuous with each other."[19] Deconstruction is an immanent subversion, rather than an external, all-embracing reductionist treatment of phenomenological hermeneutics, just as it tries to effect the same relation of immanent subversion to Structuralism, and so forth.[20] One may, in fact, see Deconstruction as an exuberant or desperate (depending on the mood) rescue operation designed to pry loose a linguistic humanism hopelessly caught between the Scylla of total captivity to the absolute truth and certainty of "self-presence," and the Charybdis of *anti-humanist* or "scientific" dissolution of that supposed certainty.

"Language," whether as discourse or text, is to be caught out and tripped up in its own metaphorical character precisely at the point where philosophical theorists claim recourse to a close relation between metaphor and technical concept or true meaning. In the case of the hermeneutical theory under discussion, an example of such metaphorical usage would be the phrase " 'referent' basically manifests the meaning 'in front of' the text,"[21] a turn of phrase whose strikingly spatial character in what is actually a nonspatial pattern of overall thought highlights, through its contrast to "meaning 'behind' the text," at once the distinction and the coherence between "sense" and "reference." The "referent" "in front of the text" is precisely that restorative "sense" of the reading of second naïveté, for which text and reader come to share a common referential world ("that way of perceiving reality, that mode-of-being-in-the-world which the text opens up for the intelligent reader")[22] which they cannot share in critical reading of the "meaning behind the text." Meaning "in front of the text" is a centered world of meaning made accessible and viable to an equally centered self.

In the one case ("meaning behind the text") the spatial metaphor is intended to indicate mutual absence or distance between semantic sense, real referent, and the reader's world. By contrast, the other spatial metaphor ("in front of") is supposed to indicate the overcoming of that distance without a direct—either naïve or Romantic—*mergence* of the previously distanced partners. To someone like Derrida, it is clear that even if the one metaphor ("behind" the text) comes close to accomplishing what is wanted from it (which is not to be taken for granted) an indication of distance or absence, the other ("in front of") means simply by oppositional affinity with the first. Insofar as it is supposed to indicate a significant *conceptual* pairing (distance between two linguistic "worlds" which remains while nonetheless being overcome, the reading of second naïveté), it simply spins its wheels. It is a case of "absence" supposedly being "presence" at the same time, a virtual admission of the fault that Deconstructionists espy at the foundation of the edifice of the traditional "signifier/signified" relation. The natural affinity of the second metaphor is not that of a "signifier" with a consistent, intelligible, and normative "signified" but simply that of one signifier or metaphor with another, previous one: Any "meaning" that "in front of" may have is *deferred* along a loosely connected, potentially indefinite metaphorical axis, and in the meantime it is what it is simply by displacing that from which it differs ("meaning behind the text"). It is this displacement or divestment of a signified world into the intertextuality of an indefinite sequence of signifiers—a focal insistence of the Deconstructionists—that is so apt in their critique of phenomenological hermeneutics: the "worlds" that are supposedly "disclosed" actually have the subversive, deconstructing nonreferentiality of pure metaphoricity built into them. Phenomenological hermeneutics, to Deconstructionists, is *malgré lui* a celebration of that very nonreferential purity of textual metaphoricity that it sets out to transcend. Second, naïveté, far from being explained and justified, is an illusion, a verbal pirouette.

Such instances of the hermeneutical theory's built-in susceptibility to deconstruction are crucial to the Deconstructionists' cumulative argument that the general bearing of hermeneutical theory is one for which "understanding" as self-presence is the indispensable and irreducible counterpart to textual "meaning" as linguistic presence, and vice versa. Language as signifier has life or spirit breathed into it by its immediate relation to self-presence, and that in turn allows it to take the shape of the signified, the means by which it attains meaning as referent or ontologically present truth. Conversely and simultaneously, "disclosure" is the bridge over which truth as presence in turn travels to present itself as meaning to self-presence now. To Deconstructionists, this linguistic polarity of self-presence and presence is equally endemic to hermeneutical theory when language is taken as discourse and when it is understood as written text. But, they say, precisely that polarity guarantees the actual priority of speech over writing in either version of the theory. The indispensability of understanding as self-presence builds the very notion of presence into language ineluctably and thus constitutes an assertion of speech rather than written text as the original and natural form of language, and of the text as a deformation of speech. What is already written is not a present event, as understanding what is written is; it must be raised to the level of present communicative event, and thereby the textuality of the text is reconverted (in obverse form) into speech.

To realize the deconstructive susceptibility of this self-enclosed, presence/self-presence, scheme is, Deconstructionists tell us, to learn with metaphorical force (or, to an outsider to the whole argument, exaggeration) the drastic difference between speech and writing, and indeed—in contrast to the absolute connection between speech as linguistic origin and the mode of self-presence in hermeneutical theory—of the independent *priority* of writing over speech. Such metaphorical and rhetorical vehemence alone will suffice to indicate the chasm opened up by the immanent subversion of the phenomenological theory of hermeneutics. Not the unreachable goal of a particular strategy but the instability and emptiness of an entire categorial scheme in which mutually indispensable conceptual devices sustain each other—and nothing else, is being proposed by the deconstruction of phenomenological hermeneutics. The Deconstructionists simply deny the stability of the theory's presuppositions.

If "meaning" implies absence and *difference* intead of centeredness or presence, then self-presence or "understanding"—its indispensable polar correlate in the theory—is bound to be just as hollow. Not that Deconstructionists necessarily deny the "reality" of centered selfhood, or even of experienced self-consciousness as its basic mode, after the fashion of the masters of "suspicion." Rather, strictly and simply as part of a way of explaining and justifying "interpretive" textual reading, specifically in the mode of second naïveté, this ingredient simply dissolves; like "presence," self-presence turns into absence, the absence of centeredness and of its "now," in relation to textuality and intertextuality.

One may well be sceptical about Derrida's and his followers' consignment of the *whole* Western linguistic tradition to the supposed metaphysical or "ontotheological" prioritizing of "phonocentric," and "logocentric," discourse over text and writing. But deconstruction does provide a strong case against the theory at issue. Indeed, at times it seems as if Deconstructionists, in their enthusiasm to consign philosophy to an awkward ancillary status to their own kind of literary reading, believe that Western metaphysics and philosophy of language from pre-Socratic days on were a grand and connected conspiracy aiming all along to arrive at the thought of Husserl and Heidegger, with only slightly camouflaged detours by way of Plato, the New Testament, Rousseau, and Saussure, and that the Deconstructionist duty is to smoke it out, root, and branch. In the process, and whatever its philosophical strengths and weaknesses, Deconstructionist association of Christianity (in contrast to Judaism) with ontotheology *tout court* has all the appearance of overkill, as sweeping generalizations usually do. Christianity, especially in its Reformation Protestant rather than liberal or neo-orthodox forms, is very much a "religion of the text," for which the textuality of the Bible is not systematically or metaphysically, but only in quite informal fashion, coordinated with linguistic meaning of a logocentric sort. In fact, the grammatical literalism of the "unfallen" biblical text, together with its textual autonomy from and priority over the *viva vox* of the interpretive tradition—all of which the Reformers proposed—may bear a remote resemblance (doubtless no more!) to the Deconstructionists' "textuality" and "intertextuality," which the latter have so far apparently not discerned. On the other hand, the affirmation of the textuality of the biblical text does not preclude a self-dispositioning of Christian language in other contexts that makes traditional and heavy drafts on "ontotheology" (especially in its Platonic and Neoplatonic versions). The integrity of textuality does not involve a systematic denial of ontotheology as one fit articulation among others for Christian doctrinal language. In other words, a Christian theological observer will want to resist a tendency toward global and foundational claims on behalf of inclusive theories, which Deconstructionists seem to share in practice, whatever the theory, with other theorists.

I do not propose to claim a decisive victory for the Deconstructionist subversion of phenomenological hermeneutics, nor to claim that Deconstruction is the ultimate mode of literary theory (nor, I believe, do Deconstructionists of the saner variety). Furthermore, it is obvious that Deconstruction is anything but universally helpful to a Christian reading of Christian Scripture, even though it may be useful *selectively*, just as hermeneutical theory may be similarly and modestly appropriate. (One thinks, for example, of aspects of experiential selfhood and self-understanding in the Gospel of John, in the reading of which a phenomenological interpretive scheme might have limited but significant applicability.) It is doubtful that *any* scheme for reading texts, and narrative texts in particular, and biblical narrative texts even more specifically, can serve globally and foundationally, so that the reading of biblical material would simply be a regional instance of the universal procedure. The contrary hermeneutical claim is, as we saw earlier, doubtful enough when it is judged by criteria of coherence and adequacy in regard to restorative or revised-literal reading of *New Testament* narratives. But now one also has to add that its very claim to adequate status as a universal and foundational theory justifying the restorative reading of "second naïveté" has been rendered highly dubious by the immanent subversion of its philosophical into a metaphorical turn at crucial points.

The threat to hermeneutical theory is that *either* "second naïveté" is no concept but simply a misleading term, and restorative hermeneutics explains or justifies no way of reading, *or* that if one is to hold out for anything like it, one had better invent a more adequate theory to support the claim. (Even so global, astringent, and telling a critic of Deconstruction as John Searle concedes the pertinence of Deconstructionist critique of phenomenology, especially in its Husserlian form.)[23] There is of course another option: One may want to claim that a notion similar to "second naïveté" (though not necessarily isomorphic with it) is indeed meaningful, but not because it is part of, or justified by, any general theory. But that is a position which neither hermeneutical Phenomenologists nor Deconstructionists will tolerate.

Closely interwoven with the hermeneutics of meaning-and-understanding is a position in modern liberal Christian theology, for which proper theological articulation has always to be the fruit of careful coordination of present cultural self-understanding, that is, a phenomenology of the contemporary cultural life-world, with an interpretation of the normative self-understanding inherent in Christianity, its sources, traditions, and historically varying external manifestations.[24] A paradoxical challenge now awaits the attention of this theology. Its proponents are understandably anxious to grasp the present intellectual, cultural, and spiritual "situation" (understood as possessing a kind of cohesive, describable essence) in its distinctiveness and its latest shape, as it may just be crafting the future immediately ahead of us. Hence, there are frequent references to the present situation as "post-modern," "post-critical," "post-theological," and so on. One may well entertain serious doubts about the wisdom of this procedure as a basic and systematic theological strategy. But that issue aside, in the context of our discussion the challenge now to the advocates of this theology of coordination or correlation is to consider seriously the possibility that the present cultural situation is among other things a *post-hermeneutical* and no longer a hermeneutical situation, and to frame their hermeneutical outlook in accordance with it, both for the sake of the technical credibility of hermeneutical theory and for the broader purpose of the cultural credibility of the theology itself.

Up to now this challenge has gone unmet among the theory's theological advocates; they have seen no need for serious modification of their views. Characteristically, they consider the possibility of such powerful high-cultural symptoms as deconstruction, or Foucault's elimination of interior unity in historiography in favor of "systems of dispersion,"[25] as well as many other basic orientations toward the relation between selfhood and culture differing drastically from that proposed under the rubrics of phenomenology, only to return to their previous analytical fruits. One way or another, the normative permanence of unique, irreducible, and shared interior experience remains the basic ingredient in any cultural life-world they discover. The depictions offered by other options may be temporary interruptions in that field of vision, but they are never potentially basic disturbers or immanent threats to this remarkably assured view of the compatibility of self-understanding with an analysis of apparently any present cultural situation. In the end, drastically "other" options usually become coopted—illustrations despite themselves both of the need for the phenomenological agenda and its perennial discoveries.

Just as in hermeneutical and phenomenological theory "understanding" as an event of self-presence remains a basically unquestioned category, and a cultural world is always a particular collective understanding, so in the theory's cultural-theological version religious experience or something like it remains a serenely assured category with an ever pertinent, ever available cultural correlate in every situation, including that which is post-hermeneutical or post-religious. So, for example, in the words of David Tracy, "We must keep alive the sense of the uncanny—the post-religious, religious sense of our situation."[26] It seems never really to have been in question in the first place.

III.   Prospects for the Literal Sense

What of the future of the "literal reading"? The less entangled in theory and the more firmly rooted not in a narrative (literary) tradition but in its primary and original context, a religious community's "rule" for faithful reading, the more clearly it is likely to come into view, and the stronger as well as more flexible and supple it is likely to look. From that perspective, a theory confined to describing how and in what specific kind of context a certain kind of reading functions is an improvement over the kind of theoretical endeavor that tries to justify its very possibility in general.

Hermeneutical theory obviously belongs to the latter kind, but so also do those arguments for and against the historical factuality of the (perhaps!) history-like or literal and (perhaps!) historical narratives of the Bible that have generated so much religious and scholarly heat since the eighteenth century. As arguments claiming general validity they have usually been governed on both sides by the assumptions that "meaning" is identical with "possible truth," and that if a story belongs to the genre of history-like or "realistic" narrative, its meaning *qua* possible truth belongs to the class called "factuality." The necessary obverse is that if stories are *not* judgeable by this criterion, they are finally not realistic but belong to some other genre and therefore make a different kind of truth claim. (This is finally the cutting edge of the reading of the New Testament by the proponents of the "second naïveté" of "restorative" hermeneutics. In their reading, the "historicity" of human being and human narratives "discloses" the truth and reality of a secondary and transcendent world that differs totally from the narrative description, transforming the latter into metaphor instead. Hence their preference in the synoptic Gospels for the metaphorical and disclosive character of the parables over the realistic, literally descriptive character of the passion and resurrection narratives.)

A recent proposal in the argument about the mutual bearing of realistic narrative and historical fact claim in respect of biblical stories, especially the synoptic Gospels, represents a transition from a high-powered to a less ambitious kind of general theorizing. It holds that the Gospel stories as well as large portions of Old Testament narrative are indeed "realistic," but that the issue of their making or not making factual or, for that matter, other kinds of truth claims is not part of the scope of hermeneutical inquiry. "Meaning" in this view is logically distinct from "truth," even where the two bear so strong a family resemblance as the designations "history-like" and "historical" imply. The factuality or nonfactuality of at least some of these narratives, important as it is no doubt in a larger religious or an even more general context, involves a separate argument from that concerning their meaning.[27]

Two related assumptions are implied when this move is made as part of a plea on behalf of realistic or literal (as well as figural) reading. First, there is a suspension of the question whether "truth" is a general class (over and above specific true items), to which all reasonable people have equal access as a set of proper conclusions drawn from credible grounds, by way of rational procedures common to all (except that, unlike myself, not everybody has found right reason yet). But second, "meaning," unlike "truth," *can* be affirmed to be such a general class allowing across-the-board access to all reasonable people who know how to relate genus, species, and individual case properly. One appeals first to a qualitatively distinct genus of text (and meaning) called "literary" and then argues both historically and in principle that within it there is a species called "realistic narrative" that is quite distinct from, say, romance or heroic epic. To this species then, biblical narrative is said to belong; indeed it is often said to be its original and paradigm.[28]

The resemblance of this view to Anglo-American "New Criticism" is obvious and has often been pointed out. Both claim that the text is a normative and pure "meaning" world of its own which, quite apart from any factual reference it may have, and apart from its author's intention or its reader's reception, stands on its own with the authority of self-evident intelligibility. The reader's "interpretation" can, and indeed has to be, minimal, reiterative, and formal, so that the very term "interpretation" is already misleadingly high-powered. "Criticism" is a far more appropriate term because it is more low-keyed and leaves the text sacrosanct, confining itself to second-order analysis, chiefly of the formal stylistic devices which are the "literary" body of the text. In the case of the "realistic" novel these are devices such as temporal structuring, the irreducible interaction of character and plot, ordinary or "mixed" rather than elevated style, and so forth. These devices are said to be of the very essence of the text and of its quality as a linguistic sacrament, inseparable from the world that it is (rather than merely represents), but also the means by which that world is rendered to the reader so that (s)he can understand it without any large-scale "creative" contribution of his/her own.

This outlook is less high-powered than hermeneutical theory, not only because it is confined to "meaning" as logically distinct from "truth" but because the formal features of realistic narrative about which it generalizes are as often as not implicit rather than explicit, so that they must be *exhibited* in textual examples rather than *stated* in abstract terms. But even though less high-powered, general theory it remains: The Gospel narratives "mean" realistically because that is the general literary class to which they belong. But precisely in respect of generalizing adequacy this theory has grave weaknesses. First, the claim to the self-subsistence or self-referentiality of the text apart from any true world is as artificial as it may (perhaps!) be logically advantageous: Moreover, the view is usually not held consistently, for New Critics argue not only for the integrity but the truth of their approach when challenged by contrary reductionist views such as Historicism, Structuralism, or Deconstruction. Despite their anti- or non-philosophical bearing, in fact many of them espouse a theory of a purely aesthetic kind of truth in literature. Second, it is similarly artificial and dubious to claim a purely external relation of text and reading, which in effect sets aside the mutual implication of interpretation and textual meaning (as hermeneutical theorists would have it) or of reading and the textuality of the text (in terms of the Deconstructionists). If a narrative or a poem should "not mean but be," avoiding paraphrase as the proper means to the realization of this ideal comes close to enthroning verbal repetition as the highest form of understanding.

In short, the less high-powered general theory that upholds the literal or realistic reading of the Gospels may be just as perilously perched as its more majestic and pretentious hermeneutical cousin. There is a greater problem yet with the more modest view. The resemblance of New Criticism to, indeed its partial derivation from, Christian theology (especially Aristotelian modes of that theology) has often and rightly been pointed out. Endowing the text with the stature of complete and authoritative embodiment of "truth" in "meaning," so that it is purely and objectively self-referential, is a literary equivalent of the Christian dogma of Jesus Christ as incarnate Son of God, the divine Word that is one with the bodied person it assumes. Here is a general theory about texts of which the paradigm case is not only in the first instance not textual but, more important, is itself the *basis* rather than merely an *instance* of the range as well as cohesion of meaning and truth in terms of which it is articulated. It has always been clear in Christian tradition that if the truth of such a dogma as that of the incarnation is to be affirmed, it has to be done by faith rather than rational demonstration. Less evident but equally true is that if the dogma is to be held consistently, its very *meaning*, that is, its logical as well as onto-logical conceivability is a matter of faith, and therefore of reason strictly in the mode of faith seeking understanding. Suppose one affirms that a partial but fitting second-order redescription of the Gospel narratives may be carried out under the general and distinct ontological categories of infinite or divine and finite. or human "natures" (and there is no reason to think that this set of categories is either worse or better than a number of others for what may aptly, if modestly, be termed "interpretation" of the dogma): The implicit rule of religious use or "rule of faith" under which it will be done is that the conceivability of the unity of the two categories in personal ascription, without compromise to their distinctness *qua* categories, is dependent on the *fact* of that unity. Conversely, then, it has to be denied that the fact is logically dependent on the conceivability of the categories' unification. All descriptive endeavors to show didactically or abstractly, rather than to reiterate narratively, *how* the unity is such as not to compromise the categories' distinction, or how they are inherently fit for unification, will break down or else, a better alternative, remain incomplete. The "rule" for the statement of the dogma and the deployment of categories in the process will therefore always have a reserved or negative cast: Nothing must be said in the proper philosophical articulation of the dogma such that the rightful priority of the categories' coherence in unitary personal ascription over their abiding logical distinctness would jeopardize the integrity of the latter. The implication of this reserve is that the full, *positive explanation* of the rule's rational status, while not at all an inappropriate aim, will have to await another condition than our present finitude. For now, the faith articulated in the dogma is, under this assumption, indeed not irrational, "paradoxi-cal" or "fideistic," but rather rational yet fragmentary. The formal statement of the dogma's logic is of a (modestly) transcendental sort.

The irony of New Criticism (and it is not the first instance of this kind) is to have taken this specific case and rule and to have turned them instead into a general theory of meaning, literature, and even culture, in their own right. Detached from the original that is the actual, indispensable ground and subject matter of its meaning, the specific rule is turned about instead into its very opposite, a scheme embracing a whole class of general meaning constructs, from a Christian culture (in the religiously imperialistic and more than mildly fantasizing visions of T. S. Eliot's cultural-theological writings) to genres of literature. They are all understood "incarnationally" or "sacramentally." As a result, the original of this process of derivation, the doctrine of the incarnation of the Word of God in the person and destiny of Jesus of Nazareth, has now become an optional member within the general class, in which those who subscribe to the class may or may not wish to believe.

There may or may not be a class called "realistic narrative," but to take it as a general category of which the synoptic Gospel narratives and their partial second-order redescription in the doctrine of the Incarnation are a dependent instance is first to put the cart before the horse and then cut the lines and claim that the vehicle is self-propelled. The realistic novel, in which history-likeness and history prey on each other in mutual puzzlement concerning the reality status of each and their relation (so that Balzac could claim that his novels are true history, while Truman Capote could invent a category called the nonfictional novel for his reports on a series of gruesome murders in rural Kansas) is, from the perspective of the rule of faith and its interpretive use in the Christian tradition, nothing more than an appropriate even if puzzling as well as incomplete analogy or "type" of their "anti-type," the coherence between linguistic or narrative and real worlds rendered in the Gospel stories. In that tradition, the ascriptive literalism of the story, the *history-likeness* if you will, of the singular agent enacting the unity of human finitude and divine infinity, Jesus of Nazareth, is taken to be itself the ground, guarantee, and conveyance of the truth of the depicted enactment, its *historicity* if you will—if, that is, in the wake of the Enlightenment these are the categories of descriptive meaning and referential truth one wishes to employ. The linguistic, textual world is in this case not only the *necessary* basis for our orientation within the real world, according to the Christian claims about this narrative, and this narrative alone; it is also *sufficient* for the purpose. This is hardly the sort of claim which one would want to turn into one instance of a general class, either in historical theory or theory of the novel, even if it is an antitype to serve a host of imperfect, partial types.

Whatever one may think of the phenomenologists' hermeneutical theory, it *is* a general theory; however, under its auspices the literal reading of the Gospel narratives vanishes, both because in application the theory revises it into incoherence and out of existence, and because the theory *qua* theory cannot persuasively make good on its claim to the availability of the revisionary literalism of a "second naïveté." As for the New Criticism, a literal reading of the Gospels is appropriate under its auspices, but only because and to the extent that it is in fact a disguised Christian understanding of them and not a reading under a general theory, not even a more low-level theory of meaning than the general hermeneutical scheme.

Rather than an example of an explanatory theory of meaning at work on the status and possibility of a specific case under its auspices, what we have in the *sensus literalis* is a reading about which one needs to say first that it governs and bends to its own ends whatever general categories it shares—as indeed it has to share— with other kinds of reading (e.g., "meaning," "truth," as well as their relation). It is a case-specific reading which may or may not find reduced analogues elsewhere. Second, it is not only case-specific but as such belongs first and foremost into the context of a sociolinguistic community, that is, of the specific religion of which it is part, rather than into a literary ambience. Both considerations involve lowering our theoretical sights yet further to the level of mere description rather than explanation, to the specific set of texts and the most specific context, rather than to a general class of texts ("realistic narrative") and the most general context ("human experience").

That exercise in self-restraint should not be difficult to state, despite the complexity of the exposition up to this point. Nor does it preclude inquiry into either the fact or the character of possible truth claims involved in the literal reading of the Gospels. It is simply an acknowledgment of the inescapably ambiguous or problematic *philosophical* status of such claims when they are analyzed under the auspices of general theories. The theoretical task compatible with the literal reading of the Gospel narratives is that of describing how and in what context it functions. In that regard we need to do little more than return to the beginning of the essay: Established or "plain" readings are warranted by their agreement with a religious community's rules for reading its sacred text. It is at best questionable that they are warranted, except quite provisionally, under any other circumstances: Theories of realistic narrative for example are not likely to be highly plausible except in tandem with an informal cultural consensus that certain texts have the quasi-sacred and objective literary status of "classics," which form the core of a broader literary "canon." The plausibility structure in this case is a literary imitation of a religious community's authority structure; it rests on a tradition, reinforced by communal, usually professional, agencies authorized to articulate the consensus about what is to be included within the canon and what is to be especially exalted within that privileged group as "classic." The pleas by advocates of phenomenological hermeneutics that the status of a "classic" is warranted when a work provides a "realized experience of that which is essential, that which endures"[29] is little more than a tacit acknowledgment that the temporary cultural consensus is already on the wane, and agreed upon or "plain" readings with it. As a warranting argument it is a last-ditch holding operation, no matter how sound it may be as a report of how people are likely to experience works that already (or still) have the cultural status of classics.

In the tradition of Christian religion and its communal life, scripture has played many parts; it has been a guide to life, an inspiration to heart and mind, a norm for believing. The (largely but not wholly) informal set of rules under which it has customarily been read in the community, in the midst of much disagreement about its contents, has been fairly flexible and usually not too constrictive. The *minimal* agreement about reading the Scriptures (as distinct from their status or scope) has been as follows: First, Christian reading of Christian Scriptures must not deny the literal ascription to Jesus, and not to any other person, event, time or idea, of those occurrences, teachings, personal qualities and religious attributes associated with him in the stories in which he plays a part, as well as in the other New Testament writings in which his name is invoked. This ascription has usually also included the indirect referral to him of that "Kingdom of God," the parabolic proclamation of which is attributed to him in the texts, and of which he himself was taken to be (in a phrase of Austin Farrer's) the "self-enacted parable" both in word and deed. Second, no Christian reading may deny either the unity of Old and New Testaments or the congruence (which is not by any means the same as literal identity) of that unity with the ascriptive literalism of the Gospel narratives. Third, any readings not in principle in contradiction with these two rules are permissible, and two of the obvious candidates would be the various sorts·of historical-critical and literary readings.

Whether or not there are exact parallels in other religions to this sort of governed use of scriptures for the edification, practical guidance, and orientation in belief of the members, it is at least a typical ingredient in a recognizably religious pattern.[30]

In days long past, observers used to put the practices and beliefs of differing "high" religions side by side, in order to compare and contrast discrete items such as the nature of the divine or the character of salvation. This procedure rightly came to be seen as naïve and wooden because it ignored questions of the criteria for comparison. The result of the quest for criteria was a rash of theories of the relation of religion to human nature, to the character of society, to the course of human history at large (are religion and history evolutionary?) or to the specific host or guest cultures with which specific religions intertwined (are religions unique and relative and therefore incomparable because cultures are?). The strength of phenomenology of religion has been to propose a new option: While there is an irreducibly self-identical, universal "essence" of religion, it is not found in the empirically given surface data or manifestations of religion—which remain culture-specific—but in the depth experience of which they are the symbolic forms. That essence or quality has to be adduced from them but is in fact logically prior to them. Religion is pre-cognitive, it is at home in the transcendental dimension in which selves apprehend themselves by way of the indispensable instrumentalities of culture (art, ritual, myth, etc.). In contrast to other ways of seeing religion, this outlook is able to appreciate both the unity and diversity in the spectrum of the world's religions, always of course on the twin assumptions of the priority of the unity and its transcendental or experiential character: To understand the unitary essence of religion is identical with being, in however attenuated a form, religious.

Scepticism about this view—its assignment of primordial status to the self and its experience, its claim to a native religious cohabitation of the self and "the sacred" or "transcendent," the unpersuasiveness of its hermeneutical ventures—need not entail a return to understanding religions as the products either of identical mechanisms in institutional behavior patterns or of distinctive and therefore incomparable cultures. With phenomenologists one may agree that religions (and cultures, for that matter) are personal and interpersonal activities—even if not perhaps primarily experiences—rather than impersonal or superpersonal entities with independent causal powers, without adhering to a strongly developed general theory of the self or of understanding in phenomenological fashion. At the same time one may agree with interpretive social scientists who hold that a "culture" (including a religion) is like a language, a multi-level communicative network that forms the indispensably enabling context for persons to enact both themselves and their mutual relations. As in the case of phenomenology concerning selfhood, so in the case of social science concerning culture, it is best to postpone the generalizing tendency that raises theory from the descriptive to the explanatory power. ("Reductive" explanation of cultures and especially religions may or may not be compatible with interpretation or exposition from a merely descriptive point of view; the point is that it is a transition to a very different and generalizing stage of reflection. One only has to take care that the integrity and complexity of the description does not get lost in the transition. Reductive theoreticians, or masters and disciples of "suspicion" are usually better at starting at a point past the transition and looking back than at actually making or explaining the transition.)

The descriptive context, then, for the *sensus literalis* is the religion of which it is part, understood at once as a determinate code in which beliefs, ritual, and behavior patterns, ethos as well as narrative, come together as a common semiotic system, and also as the community which is that system in use—apart from which the very term ("semiotic system") is in this case no more than a misplaced metaphor. Clifford Geertz calls culture an "acted document," and the term applies also to religion.[31] Geertz calls the low-level theoretical effort at describing culture, which we have also affirmed for religion, "thick description" (using a term of Gilbert Ryle's). It is, first, description of details as parts of "interworked systems of construable signs . . . within which they can be intelligibly . . . described."[32] Second, it is description from the actor's, participant's, or language user's point of view, yet without mimicry or confusion of identity on the part of the interpreter.[33]

Those who follow this low-level use of theory for "placing" religions as symbol systems are persuaded that the description and critical appraisal of a religion from within the religious community itself, and external "thick" description, while certainly not identical, are not wholly disparate. Yet their congruence does not require—on the contrary it eschews—the elaborate synthesizing requirements of a more general, explanatory theory. To understand a religion or a culture to which one is not native does not demand a general doctrine of the core of humanity, selfhood, and the grounds of inter-subjective experience. There is of course the need for normal human sensitivity and respect. But beyond that, in Geertz's words:

> Whatever accurate sense one gets of what one's informants are "really like" comes . . . from the ability to construe their modes of expression, what I would call their symbol systems. . . . Understanding the form and pressure of . . . natives' inner lives is more like grasping a proverb, catching an allusion, seeing a joke—or . . . reading a poem—than it is like achieving communion.[34]

This is understanding without "empathy" or "transcultural identification with our subjects."[35] George Lindbeck has called this low-level theoretical deployment in the analysis of religions a "cultural linguistic approach" to the topic,[36] and has used the term "intratextual" to describe the kind of theology—the "normative explication of the meaning a religion has for its adherents"—that is not identical but congruent with it.[37] The congruence lies in the persuasion that

Meaning is constituted by the uses of a specific language rather
than being distinguishable from it. Thus the proper way to determine what "God" signifies, for example, is by examining how the
word operates in a religion and thereby shapes reality and experience rather than by first establishing its propositional or experiential meaning and reinterpreting or reformulating its uses accordingly.[38]

"Intratextuality" in many of the "high" religions is used not only
in an extended or metaphorical but in a literal sense, for they are in
varying degrees "religions of the (or a) book." "They all have
relatively fixed canons of writings that they treat as exemplary or
normative instantiations of their semiotic codes. One test of faith-
fulness for all of them is the degree to which descriptions corre-
spond to the semiotic universe paradigmatically encoded in holy
writ."[39]

The direction in the flow of intratextual interpretation is that of
absorbing the extratextual universe into the text, rather than the
reverse (extratextual) direction. The literal sense is the paradigmatic
form of such intratextual interpretation in the Christian community's use of its scripture: The literal ascription to Jesus of Nazareth of
the stories connected with him is of such far-reaching import that it
serves not only as focus for inner-canonical typology but reshapes
extratextual language in its manifold descriptive uses into a typological relation to these stories. The reason why the intratextual
universe of this Christian symbol system is a narrative one is that a
specific set of texts, which happen to be narrative, has become
primary, even within scripture, and has been assigned a literal
reading as their primary or "plain" sense. They have become the
paradigm for the construal not only of what is inside that system but
for all that is outside. They provide the interpretive pattern in terms
of which *all* of reality is experienced and read in this religion. Only
in a secondary or derivative sense have they become ingredient in a
general and literary narrative tradition. The latter is actually not
only a provisional but a highly variable set of contexts for these
texts; it is not foundational for their meaning, and there is no
intrinsic reason to suppose that any given general theory for their
reading in that context, be it hermeneutical or anti-hermeneutical,

ought to be assigned pride of place—including that of New Criticism with its logical dependence on Christian theology. Equally clearly it is once more a case of putting the cart before the horse—but this time the wagon is theological rather than literary—if one constructs a general and inalienable human quality called "narrative" or "narrativity," within which to interpret the Gospels and provide foundational warrant for the possibility of their existential and ontological meaningfulness. The notion that Christian theology is a member of a general class of "narrative theology" is no more than a minor will-o'-the-wisp.

"Meaning" in a cultural-linguistic and intratextual interpretive frame is the skill that allows ethnographer and native to meet in mutual respect; if they happen to be the same person, it is the bridge over which (s)he may pass from one shore to the other and undertake the return journey; if they are natives from different tribes, it is the common ground that is established as they learn each other's languages, rather than a known precondition for doing so.

To return to the beginning: The third of these tasks is perhaps the most immediately pressing for Christian interpretation and for the future of its use of the literal sense. For the next-door neighbor to Christianity in all its various forms is Judaism with its own diversity, and they share those parts of a common scripture which Christianity has usurped from Judaism. The most pressing question from this vantage point is not the fate of the literal sense in the event of a new, perhaps more nearly universal, spiritual truth that would also constitute a new literal reading and threaten to reduce the Christian reading of the New Testament to exoteric, carnal status. This is unlikely, for we have noted that religions are specific symbol systems and not a single, high-culture reproduction of symbol-neutral eternal "truth." Lessing's "eternal gospel" is a noble ideal, but his appropriation of a story form for the purpose of advocating historical and religious progress is not a supplanting of one scriptural narrative by a later and better one; it is instead the substitution of a philosophy of history for an intratextual interpretive scheme.

A far more urgent issue for Christian interpretation is the unpredictable consequences of learning the "language" of the Jewish tradition, including the nearest Jewish equivalent to Christian literal reading. To discover Midrash in all its subtlety and breadth of options and to understand *peshat* (the traditional sense)[40] may well be to begin to repair a series of contacts established and broken time and again in the history of the church, whenever linguistic and textual Old Testament issues became pressing in intra-Christian debate. Perhaps the future may be better than the past as a result of the intervening period of liberal scholarship and the persuasion that the two religions, even though closely intertwined, are quite distinct, each with its own integrity. The convergence of distinctness and commensurability between them has yet to be discovered, and attention to Midrash and to the literal sense may play a significant part in the discovery.

In addition to the inter-religious enrichment for which one may hope from such joint inquiry, certainly for Christianity, the secular gains may be surprisingly large, even if strictly speaking incidental or secondary. The Protestant theologian Friedrich Schleiermacher called Judaism a fossil religion, in part at least out of the animus which many Rationalist, Romantic, and Idealistic thinkers bore toward Jewish particularism. And yet it is now conceivable that that "fossil" may bear more of the future of the culture of the West in its hands than Christianity, and its traditional, particularistic forms may not be adventitious to the fact. Cultural, religious, and historical parallels are dangerous and speculative. Nonetheless there may be a lesson here, at least to the effect that the relation between Christianity and Judaism—including the complex issues of the relation between their Scriptures and scriptural interpretations— may play an indispensable part in the process of Christian recovery of its own intratextual or self-description. Whether with or without the aid of such a discussion, the most fateful issue for Christian self-description is that of regaining its autonomous vocation as a religion, after its defeat in its secondary vocation of providing ideological coherence, foundation, and stability to Western culture. Beyond that, however, the example of Judaism in the modern Western world might be a beacon to a reconstituted Christian community. One never knows what this community might then contribute once again to that culture or its residues, including its political life, its quest for justice and freedom—and even its literature. If the priori-

ties are rightly ordered, the literal sense may be counted on to play a significant part in such a less pretentious enterprise. It will stretch and not break.

NOTES

1. Cf. Robert Scholes and Robert Kellogg, *The Nature of Narrative* (New York: Oxford University Press, 1960), pp. 50ff.
2. Cf. Mircea Eliade, *Patterns in Comparative Religion* (Cleveland: World, 1963), ch. I, *inter multa alia*.
3. Cf. Northrop Frye, *The Great Code: The Bible and Literature* (New York: Harcourt, Brace, Jovanovich, 1982), pp. 31ff.
4. James S. Preus, *From Shadow to Promise. Old Testament Interpretation from Augustine to the Young Luther* (Cambridge, Mass.: Harvard University Press, 1969).
5. G. E. Lessing, "The Education of the Human Race," *Lessing's Theological Writings*, translated and introduced by Henry Chadwick (Stanford: Stanford University Press, 1967), p. 96. The same message is of course a large part of the parable of the rings in Lessing's *Nathan The Wise*.
6. Cf. Frank Kermode, *The Genesis of Secrecy. On the Interpretation of Narrative* (Cambridge, Mass.: Harvard University Press, 1979), pp. 18ff., 45ff., 143ff., *passim*.
7. Paul Ricoeur, *Interpretation Theory: Discourse and the Surplus of Meaning* (Fort Worth: Texas Christian University Press, 1976), pp. 12ff.
8. Ibid., p. 12.
9. Cf. Paul Ricoeur, "Toward a Hermeneutic of the Idea of Revelation," *Essays on Biblical Interpretation*, ed. Lewis S. Mudge (Philadelphia: Fortress Press, 1980), pp. 73–118.
10. David Tracy, *Blessed Rage for Order. The New Pluralism in Theology* (New York: Seabury Press, 1975), p. 221.
11. *Semeia 4: Paul Ricoeur on Biblical Hermeneutics*, ed. J. D. Crossan (Missoula, Mont.: Scholars Press, 1975), p. 32.
12. Ibid., pp. 127ff.
13. Paul Ricoeur, "The Narrative Function," *Hermeneutics and the Human Sciences*, ed. and tr. by J. B. Thompson (New York: Cambridge University Press, 1981), p. 292.
14. Cf. ibid., pp. 293ff.
15. Tracy, op. cit., p. 206. Cf. supra, pp. 102–115 for a statement of the issue.
16. Tracy's statement of the matter, op. cit., pp. 205–207, is quite typical. If the tenor of the passage quoted above (note 10) is to turn 'Jesus' into an

allegory of "universal meaningfulness" in the shape of an event or disclosure (cf. ibid., p. 106), Tracy's subsequent *The Analogical Imagination. Christian Theology and the Culture of Pluralism* (New York: Crossroad, 1981), part II, chs. 6 and 7, tends to redress the balance and stress 'Jesus' as the unsurpassable ascriptive subject of the narratives manifesting and proclaiming the "Christ event" as an event "from God." However, since that event qua event must always be a "present experience," the movement toward universal meaningfulness as the referent of the stories and thus toward the allegorical use of 'Jesus' begins again right away (cf. ibid., p. 234, passim). It is not at all clear that Tracy's hermeneutical procedure manages to coordinate these two simultaneous referents, but what *is* clear is that if their coordination is indeed a problem and as a result one becomes the chief referent and the other its satellite, then it is the tendency toward allegorization that receives Tracy's favorable nod.

17. Paul Ricoeur, "The Model of the Text: Meaningful Action Considered as a Text," P. Rabinow and W. M. Sullivan (eds.), *Interpretive Social Science* (Berkeley: University of California Press, 1979), p. 98.

18. Ibid.

19. Terry Eagleton, *Literary Theory, An Introduction* (Minneapolis: University of Minnesota Press, 1983), p. 108.

20. Cf. Christopher Norris, *Deconstruction. Theory and Practice* (London and New York: Methuen, 1982), p. 31.

21. Tracy, *Blessed Rage for Order*, p. 51, passim.

22. Ibid.

23. John Searle, "The World Turned Upside Down." *The New York Review of Books*, XXX, 16, October 27, 1983, pp. 74–79.

24. Cf. Tracy, *The Analogical Imagination,* p. 340.

25. Michel Foucault, *The Archaeology of Knowledge* (Harper Torchbook, 1972), pp. 37f.

26. Tracy, *The Analogical Imagination*, p. 362. For Tracy's remarks about Derrida, cf. ibid., pp. 117ff., 220ff. (note 17), 361ff., passim.

27. This position is implied by the present writer in *The Eclipse of Biblical Narrative* (New Haven: Yale University Press, 1974), and made explicit in *The Identity of Jesus Christ* (Philadelphia: Fortress Press, 1975).

28. The classic statement of this case is Erich Auerbach, *Mimesis. The Representation of Reality in Western Literature* (Princeton: Princeton University Press, 1953).

29. Tracy, *The Analogical Imagination*, p. 108.

30. For an interesting parallel see Gerhard Böwering, *The Mystical Vision of Existence in Classical Islam* (Berlin and New York: Walter de Gruyter, 1980), pp. 140ff.

31. Clifford Geertz, *The Interpretation of Cultures* (New York: Basic Books, 1973), p. 10.

32. Ibid., p. 13.
33. Ibid., pp. 13, 27.
34. Geertz, "From the Native's Point of View: On the Nature of Anthropological Understanding," P. Rabinow and W. M. Sullivan (eds.), op. cit., pp. 240ff.
35. Ibid., p. 226.
36. George A. Lindbeck, *The Nature of Doctrine: Religion and Theology in a Postliberal Age* (Philadelphia: Westminster Press, 1984), pp. 32ff. I wish to acknowledge my profound indebtedness to this book and to its author.
37. Ibid., p. 113.
38. Ibid., p. 114.
39. Ibid., p. 116.
40. Cf. Raphael Loewe, "The 'Plain' Meaning of Scripture in Early Jewish Exegesis," *Papers of the Institute of Jewish Studies in London I* (Jerusalem, 1964), pp. 140–185, esp. pp. 180ff.

The Argument about Canons

FRANK KERMODE

Except when the true ecclesiastical canons are their topic, people who use the word "canon" usually have in mind quite practical issues. They may, for example, be stating that there is for students of literature a list of books or authors certified by tradition or by an institution as worthy of intensive study and required reading for all who may aspire to professional standing within that institution. Or they may be disputing the constitution of the canon, or even the right of the institution to certify it. And now the issues grow more theoretical. For some maintain that the very concept of "literature" as a way of discriminating between more and less privileged texts is an illicit one; so, *a fortiori*, further discriminations between texts that have thus been set apart must also be improper.

There are arguments of this kind now actively in progress in the humanities, and especially in literary criticism, but it is presumably acknowledged by all parties that the analogy which permits them to speak of secular canons is an imperfect one. The ecclesiastical canons are, allowing for a small measure of sectarian variation, fixed; and their fixity, however come by, is a matter of principle or doctrine. Secular canons need to be more permeable; new works are occasionally added, old works, now held to have been neglected, are revived and inserted; now and again something may be excluded. Still, even allowing for these differences, the concept of a secular canon has real force, and may even be necessary to the preservation of our disciplines. However, that is not my present subject. I want rather to see if laymen have anything to learn from listening in to a current dispute over the true character of the ecclesiastical canon, on the ideas of which their own notions of canonicity are founded.

I won't attempt to give a detailed account of what is inevitably a complicated matter, or to provide a history of the whole contention. It will be quite enough, I think, to explain the nature of the differences between the champions of the two parties that now oppose each other. What is called "canonical criticism" can fairly be represented by Professor Brevard S. Childs of Yale, and the most powerful enemy of this new style in Professor James Barr of Oxford.

Childs, in his *Introduction to the Old Testament as Scripture* (1979) says that the Bible should be treated as a "collection with parameters" (p. 40). That is, of course, the old way of treating it; but Childs says that the traditional concept of canon, weakened already by the Reformation, suffered progressive collapse under the pressure of the historical criticism that has flourished over the past two centuries. Attention was diverted from the wholeness of the Bible and directed instead to the study of individual books and segments. To criticism of this kind the canon was interesting, if at all, because of the peculiar, historically irrelevant, and inevitably misleading way it was put together. No time or energy was left for what came to be seen as a merely pious or archaic study of this fortuitously assembled collection as a unity, as the singular Bible that evolved out of the plural *biblia*.

Consequently, says Childs, there is a "long-established tension between the canon and criticism" (meaning the "traditio-historical" variety so long dominant). He wishes to reduce this tension; he will try "to understand the Old Testament as canonical scripture [that is, to see it as a literary and presumably theological unit, 'with fixed parameters'] and yet to make full and consistent use of the historical-critical tools" (p. 45). He is not, that is to say, proposing a primitivistic return to the pre-historical mode of criticism, which could afford to treat the canon as all of a piece, and divinely instituted exactly as it was; for proper attention to the integrity of the canon need not preclude historical study of the interaction between the developing corpus and the community as it changes through history. It is important to Childs that the canon was the product of many successive decisions, not of some belated and extrinsic act of validation. The history of the formation of the canon is important. Nevertheless, the canon as it is, in its full, valid form, ought, in his opinion, to be the prime object of attention.

Perhaps one can best illustrate the desired interplay between this kind of history and this kind of canonical criticism by citing the well known demonstration, by James A. Sanders in his pioneering book *Torah and Canon* (1972) that the intrusion of Deuteronomy between Numbers and Joshua decisively affected the tradition and gave a new cast to subsequent understanding of the Jewish Bible as a whole. Similar observations have been made, though with less confidence, concerning the decision to put St. John after St. Luke, so dividing the two-part work Luke and Acts.

The suggestion, then, is that historical and canonical criticism can live together and cooperate. But priority is still to be accorded to the canon. That, however, is a decision unacceptable in principle to historians who think the canon a late and arbitrary imposition with no bearing on the true (that is, the original) import of its members. Hence the tension Childs seeks to resolve. On the one hand it is necessary to maintain that the canon is not just an opaque wrapping that must be seen through or removed if one is to get at the contents and achieve a true sense of each of them. On the other, it has to be acknowledged that the constituents of the canon have their own histories, and that all the work devoted to the recovery of their original precanonical sense has not been entirely wasted.

It can of course be said that in canonical books there are words addressed to an original situation that are intended to have relevance also to later ones, and later ones that derive from, or relate more or less directly to, earlier ones, so that for some purposes at least it is only sensible to think of the canon as a whole. Moreover the preservation of old writings and the habit of venerating them happen not primarily because they are witnesses to a merely historical state of affairs, but to a state of affairs that has consuming relevance to later times; so that it is in their capacity to be *applied*, and the practice of applying them to situations other than the historical circumstances of their origin, that saves them. In a closed canon this position is generalized, and the entire body of scripture is endowed with a potential of perpetual and prophetic applicability. Before closure it was possible to obtain this necessary modern application by rewriting or adding to the body of sacred texts, but as soon as you have an enclosed canon you can no longer do that, and indeed the unalterability of the words becomes an essential aspect of its sacredness. Henceforth all interpretation, all modernisation, has to be in the form of commentary. Indeed this sequence of events is in a way repeated, since there accumulates an Oral Torah which acquires its own kind of canonicity when it is written down: and so forth. Thus in the Jewish tradition the Torah is always accompanied by its shadow, the commentary that will presumably go on for ever; and yet they are thought of together as the Torah, a syzygy of that which is fixed and that which changes in time.

Such considerations do not appear to be part of Childs's case, but he does argue that the formation of the canon was a decisive moment in the history of Jewish religion; for after that moment it was possible for Israel, no longer possessed of a Temple cult, to define itself instead in terms of a book. Its existence made possible all succeeding "actualizations" of the religion. And by minimizing the importance of the canon historical criticism has destroyed or damaged our ability to understand the process by which scriptures which were once of temporally restricted significance became one Scripture, normative for a community throughout its history.

Behind Barr's objections to Childs there is a wholly different idea of what it is to read a book, especially a book that claims or seems to claim the property of historical reference. To him it appears obvious not only that the individual books are much more important than the enclosure into which they were eventually herded, but also that what the books are *about* is much more important than the books. It is not the canon that gives the books their authority; it is the events and persons the books report. Indeed the habit of venerating writing for what it is, and for its relation with other writing that has got between the same covers, strikes him as simply dishonest, and he says so with impressive vigor. His book, *Holy Scripture: Canon, Authority and Criticism* (1983) is indeed an exceptionally strong polemic against the position taken by Childs, and against Childs himself as its leading exponent.

Barr thinks it worth notice that the interesting persons represented in the Bible got along perfectly well without a canon. Those of the New Testament, happy with their oral kerygma, were quite unaware that they were writing books that would later be made canonical. Childs had argued for a connection between the self-identity of a church and its possession of a precisely limited canon; Barr declares this connection to be illusory. How much difference, he asks, would it make to the Roman Catholic church if the book of Wisdom were struck out of the canon, and how much to the Protestant churches if they had to admit it (pp. 41–42)? Barr maintains that the extreme canonical position—that sixty-six books are inspired and nothing else is—has no scriptural support; and indeed he finds offensive the implication that there are no truths outside them, when on any sane view there are. And he points out, correctly, that to privilege books by establishing them in a canon is to confer great and in his opinion undeserved advantages upon them; for example they belong automatically—whatever their intrinsic quality—to a class above the *Confessions* of St. Augustine. Success in these matters is determined simply by getting inside; Jude is in and Augustine isn't; as with the Order of the Garter there's no damned nonsense about merit. Serious scholars should avoid such foolishness.

In any case it makes little sense, Barr believes, to speak of the Old Testament having a canon at all. The textbooks, with some support from the Talmud, will tell you it was established at the council held at Jamnia toward the end of the first century of the present era. Barr inclines to the view that if anything at all happened at Jamnia it had nothing to do with canons; perhaps there were "academic discussions about legal questions" (p. 56). Moreover he is suspicious of the so-called "Alexandrian canon", the larger canon that makes up the Greek version of the Jewish Bible. It was merely the Torah plus a number of other books. In any case, if one is really looking for the true source of authority in Judaism one will have to admit that it is not identifiable with scripture but with Torah and Talmud together; so that even if a canon were fixed at Jamnia or anywhere else, "this was a less important and less decisive fact than would seem natural to those who have seen the notion of the canon through the glass of the Calvinistic Reformation" (p. 61). It will be seen that Professor Barr has little use for canons in general. They are, if seriously taken, impediments to the real business of history.

However, his strongest objections to Childs arise less from disagreements about the history of the canon than from the claim that "canon and criticism" can be put to work as partners. This is tantamount to saying that truth and falsehood can be yoked and plough together. And the difference between Childs and Barr now presents itself in this manner: for Childs the final meaning—the meaning established by the formation of a canon—is the true one; but for Barr the true meaning is the *original* meaning, to be ascertained as far as possible by progressive historical research. Here, then, is the root of this matter: the argument is between "objective" history and a hermeneutic approach to truth.

According to Barr, "canonical" criticism entails a "decontextualization" (the stripping away, he means, of the real historical context) comparable to that effected by midrash—which updates by adaptive commentary the text that time has made obscure or apparently irrelevant—or the selfishly limited interpretative techniques used by the Qumram community, techniques which applied scripture exclusively to the modern moment of the sect (p. 80). Such decontextualization entails falsehood. Truth lies in the historical method; it is therefore dependent upon scholarly methods and techniques discovered in the past couple of hundred years. Barr allows that its discovery was belated, but holds that it has nevertheless its basis in "an ultimate datum of faith" (p. 101). These methods give us access to the important persons and events described in the books of the Bible; and to be interested in them is to be interested in the truth. But scholars whose training has been oriented toward hermeneutics, especially in the adulterated versions of the German originals he says are current in the United States, are not interested in the truth. He blows them all away with an epigram: "The final criterion for theology cannot be relevance; it can only be truth" (p. 118).

This is the position expounded by Barr in a long and acrimonious appendix. That the "final" meaning can be the true one he rejects on instinct. That "appropriation" or application is inseparable from understanding, that the most learned and conscientious historian is still restricted by his own historical situation, a situation of which he cannot be so fully conscious as to transcend it by an effort of will and intellect—these are just the arguments Barr most deplores. He says there are grounds for thinking "this philosophy" attributed to Bultmann and his epigoni—"a wrong one" (p. 143) but he doesn't, at any rate in this book, say what those grounds are. It was presumably enough to notice that the consequences of behaving as if this philosophy were a right one are absurd and repellent. What, for instance, is one to make of a way of doing biblical scholarship that treats Amos as of no more importance than his redactors? Or, more generally, that regards the Bible as a "separate cognitive zone" (p. 168)? The position is so ridiculous as to require no confutation.

Whether Barr is right about the absurdity of this view of the canon or not, he is surely wrong to call it a twentieth-century innovation. For example, it is stated dogmatically by Milton's Jesus in *Paradise Regained*, and would have seemed familiar to all who defined *curiositas* as the quest for useless knowledge, meaning knowledge not conducive to salvation: a very large number of people over a very long period. However, that is not the important issue, which I take to be, inevitably, hermeneutic. Barr asserts that it is untrue to claim that understanding and application are simultaneous; but that is the belief of the opposite party. Strong in the conviction that common sense supports only his own view, Barr simply denounces theirs. But there is more to be said.

One could reasonably say that some modern criticism is "holistic" and "appropriative"; which of course is not to say that these are exclusively modern qualities. Indeed such criticism bears an obvious resemblance to some ancient modes of interpretation. It is rather important to understand this, though it is equally important to take account of the differences between old and new. Probably the most important (as this dispute demonstrates) is that the modern variety has a strong antithetical relation to the tradition of "objective" historical scholarship which it wishes to modify or oppose. Childs of course knows that very well, and Barr accordingly scolds him for his ambivalence toward historical criticism; but it would surely, even on his view, be a worse error to forget or ignore that kind of criticism altogether and really write like the Qumram sectaries.

That there are rote denunciations of historical criticism by persons unqualified to make them, as Barr alleges, may well be true. There are always people around who think it would be a good thing

to abolish the past. Barr remarks, and plausibly, that Rudolf Bultmann, the godfather of hermeneutics as understood by most Ameri-
can theologians, would have been disgusted by such facile condem-
nations of the sort of work on which he spent so much of his life.
Evidently Barr thinks better of that side of Bultmann's work than he
does of the hermeneutics. In fact Bultmann cannot have thought of
the two as quite so easily separated; indeed the relationship between
his historical work and his hermeneutics, like the argument between
Childs and Barr, is inescapably a hermeneutic issue, and one that
already has a very long history.

The problem declared itself, and was duly discussed, as soon as
the historical criticism of the New Testament began with the work
of Semler and Michaelis in the eighteenth century. Michaelis saw
that to subject the separate books of the Bible to historical analysis
implied the view that the canon was not uniformly inspired. He did
not think this change of attitude harmful to religion; indeed he
tried—by historical research!—to establish which books were truly
inspired and which were not. But the consequences for later scholarship were very great, and the inferences drawn were different.
Scholars were able to behave as if inspiration was none of their
business, and the tensions between history and faith, reflected
sometimes in controversy between historian and theologian, and
sometimes within one man, who aspired to be both, became a
permanent problem.

Almost a century before Barr we find William Wrede confidently
stating that objective scholarship has no concern with the canon. It
must simply seek "to recover the actual state of affairs"; what
theology makes of the results is another business altogether. The
vocation of the scholar calls for complete disinterest: "he must be
able to distinguish his own thinking from that alien to it, modern
ideas from those of the past; he must be able to prevent his own
view, however dear, from exerting any influence on the object of
research, to hold it, so to speak, in suspension. For he only wishes
to discover how things really were." The words echo Ranke, and
the practice of historical scholarship continues to do so. Wrede
expressly asserts the consequences of this doctrine for the canon
when he says that the New Testament writings are not to be
understood "from the point of view of a subsequent experience

with which they *originally* had nothing whatever to do [my italics]."
There must be no difference between the ways in which one treats
canonical and non-canonical documents. The assembly into a canon
of certain favored documents is at best evidence for the quite
obsolete presuppositions or desires of canon-makers, trapped in
their own historical moment; and the assumption is that by using
modern historical methods the scientific scholar is exempted from
any such historical limitation, and may make direct contact with the
past as it really was.[1]

That there can be no distinction between sacred and secular
hermeneutics—that biblical texts are susceptible to exactly the
same treatment as any other ancient documents—was early declared
to be a rule in biblical interpretation. But it is a position easier to
assert than to maintain. If you treat the sacred book exactly like any
other you must ask, for example, what was the nature of the now
blurred original? What were the local constraints, the historical
needs, the intentions of the human author? These are matters for the
historian. The theologian, on the other hand, will have to consider
the canonical New Testament as the source of his interest and the
object of his enquiries, the very donnée of his religion. Yet the
historians are, for the most part, clerics, and wish to reconcile with
their scientific historical project the religious fore-understanding
they possess as Christian preachers. And even if these theologians
are not historians they can scarcely dare to ignore the extent and
import of centuries of historical research and speculation.

Such was the dilemma of Rudolf Bultmann. He was an eminent
practitioner of that branch of historical enquiry known as form-
criticism. He believed that the historical was the only scientific
method of research. But as a theologian, working in the shadow of
Barthian existentialism, he needed to reconcile his practice as a
historian with the assumption that faith was immediate, modern,
and personal. He summed up his attitude thus: "historical and
theological exegesis stand in a relationship that does not lend itself
to analysis, because genuine historical exegesis rests on an existential confrontation with history and therefore coincides with theological exegesis."[2]

Bultmann was therefore, it seems, committed to these opinions:
(1) that "the interpretation of biblical writings is subject to exactly

the same conditions of understanding as any other literature" a view he shared with many precursors; (2) that their interpretation depended upon fore-understandings between the reader and the text. There has to be previous acquaintance with the material—an understanding not acquired directly from the text in question, a presupposition. But what is presupposed is, at least in part, a relation between the interpreter and god. Bultmann's fore-understanding of biblical texts is therefore unavoidably theological, as of course it would not be if he were reading a secular text or indeed uncanonical religious writings. He seems, by a very tortuous route, to have got himself back into something like the position of Augustine; and the formula he uses to get out of that position will not convince everybody.

The effect of such fore-understanding as Bultmann speaks of is an easy one to illustrate. A Jew may share with a Christian the presupposition that he is concerned with the question of God, and the presupposition that the Old Testament bears on that question. But their concerns are shaped by different notions of the truth; the Jew will not think the Christian correct in his interpretation of the Jewish Bible because he reads it in the light of assumptions concerning the New Testament. A Christian—St. Augustine for example—will hold that the faithful must read the Old Testament as typological, as containing latent truths the Jews have obstinately ignored. Fore-understandings are obviously different for different religions, and they will be different again for the non-believer; but it is these fore-understandings that determine the application which, for example in Gadamer, who uses the above illustration, determines meaning.[3] Of course fore-understanding is not foreknowledge. It implies a certain provisionality in one's approach to a text, and the text will modify it; Bultmann is of course fully aware of that. But it remains clear enough that historical self-understanding (such as we get from dialogue with other people or with profane books) is, in his theology, a wholly different matter from the eschatological understanding of faith.

How then can it be that historical enquiry into sacred books should use methods identical with those proper for profane texts? Are the latter also to be read in some eschatological sense? The answer seems to be that the methods must in practice differ. There is a truth, Gadamer observes in the course of his remarks on Bultmann, which is a revealedness revealed historically to subjects historically situated; and this truth is not eternal. Bultmann wants truth to be what is understood within the existential possibilities of the interpreter, but also wants the historical facts to have a status independent of such considerations; to claim that the two positions are one is to claim more than common sense will allow. The "tension" spoken of by Childs is not so easily eliminated.

Gadamer also speaks of the "tensions" between historical study and hermeneutics. The historian is always after something *behind* the text. "He seeks in the text what the text is not, of itself, seeking to provide [evidence, for instance, of a pre-redactional state, direct testimony as to events and persons]. . . . He will always go back behind [the texts] and the meaning they express [which he will not regard as the inherently true meaning] to enquire into the reality of which they are the involuntary [*scil.* 'perhaps distorted'?] expression. Texts are set beside all the other historical material available, i.e., beside the so-called relics of the past." But the critic is interested in the *text* and *its* meaning. Hence the tensions, which of late—indeed for a long time—have been masked by the fact that literary criticism has allowed itself to be regarded as "an ancillary discipline to history."[4] (Note that for Gadamer it is the historical method that violates the intention of the *text*, whereas in recognitive hermeneutics it is held that the intention of the *author*, the sole donor of meaning, is the victim of the sophistries of Gadamer and his like.)

For Gadamer the only way to reconcile the two practices of history and criticism is to insist on the integrative role of application. And he makes in this connection a point of unusual interest. Both historian and critic assume, whether consciously or not, a need to relate individual text to a total context. The historian's fore-understanding impels him to apply the individual text to a total historical situation (or, as Barr would probably say, to the true historical context). The critic's fore-understanding makes him try to understand the text in the unity of its meaning, its total textual context (which will certainly entail intertextual relations limited only by the boundaries of a canon, if at all). In either case a prior supposition determines the application. Each such supposition has its own history and its own "situatedness." Each presupposes some sort of totality to which it must find its relation. Nobody, that is, will read only and exactly what is *there*. And of course nobody will ever again read exactly as Barr or Gadamer or any one else reads.

Gadamer likes to say that he is only describing things as they are, merely saying what is the case or the truth of the matter (though since he thinks that truth is not eternal this leaves room for disagreement from the standpoints of different fore-understandings than his, which is precisely part of the truth he is telling). And in the present instance it does appear that he is stating the facts of the matter—that either side of the Barr-Childs argument makes a large assumption about the context of its observations on texts. Gadamer, as he often rightly remarks, is not hostile to historical research, and he denies that he is opening the door to arbitrary interpretation, a common charge against him. But his view of what happens in historical research would not be acceptable to Barr. "It is part of real understanding . . . that we regain concepts of an historical past in such a way that they include our own comprehension of them. . . . There is no such thing . . . as a point outside history from which the identity of a problem can be conceived without the vicissitudes of the various attempts to solve it."[5] Moreover he might add that the presupposition that one is free of presuppositions is the consequence of many former presuppositions, which are themselves a proper study for historians, who had better look out for their own.

Neither of our combatants shows much interest in Gadamer, but since I have brought him in as an adjudicator I had better say that on the whole Childs fares better in his judgment than Barr. Not that Barr would mind; for Gadamer belongs to a tradition of hermeneutics of which Barr would say, with E. D. Hirsch, that it has simply gone off in the wrong direction, taking the scenic route via Heidegger instead of the direct Schleiermachian road. Barr has stayed on that road, preferring the objective or recognitive highway, which is why he sounds like Wrede, and why he has so little time for the canon. The Bible is an unintegrated collection of *biblia*. Considered as a whole it has no special claim on the attention of the historian. I don't think Barr ever says anything quite so confident—he seems clear that Christians have to treat the Bible, the book as assembled, differently from other books, as possessing authority—but as a man with an authoritative vocation to study history he need not, in his vocation, be disturbed by that belief.

And so it happens that Childs fares better with Gadamer. He might suffer criticism for presupposing that one particular historical act of application, namely the establishment of the canon, should be so privileged, but he could plausibly reply that the canon was not only the product of many former acts of application but the culmination of all that preceded it, and the foundation of all that were to follow; so that even in purely historical terms it is privileged.

Nevertheless, this assertion of privilege also proceeds from certain presuppositions. In forms less qualified than Childs's own but still related to his procedures, one might say that confidence in the integrity of the canon stems from a partly occult assumption that might for short be called magical. And something similar can be said of Barr. For the sake of clarity I will restate the character of the opposition between our champions in a crude and extreme manner. One party would really prefer to have the original documents, or perhaps even any oral predecessors, than the canonical texts. This, the Barr party, may be said to have a nostalgia for the pre-text, for the persons and events behind the books. Here is a touch of magic, the magical power of narrative as it is described in the opening words of *Adam Bede*: one may see in a drop of ink that which will "reveal to any chance comer far-reaching views of the past." Emulating "the Egyptian sorcerer," the author says that "with this drop of ink at the end of my pen" she "will show you the roomy workshop of Mr. Jonathan Burge, carpenter and builder, in the village of Hayslope, as it appeared on the eighteenth of June, in the year of our Lord 1799."

Persons and events will thus be made available to the reader, as if by magic. The other party is in general willing to use the history of the texts and their redactions, but only as pre-history of the text itself, a text that is fixed and calls for interpretation affirming its coherence and plenitude, with internal relations one can only with difficulty avoid describing as organic, and a complexity-in-unity inviting us to think of it as a world in itself. One side treats the text as a difficult means of access to historical truths which belong to the whole context of history. The other treats history as a precursor of a text which constitutes its own context. Each depends upon a magical presupposition.

It might be possible to argue for a third view. What about treating the canon as a stage in tradition, and then considering it as an intertextual system, only to the degree that it imposes its own measure of intertextuality? This would entail that one did not treat it as rigidly bounded, as confining the attention of serious interpreters to the 'inside' books—rejecting, that is, the "fixed parameters" of Childs, but without denying a measure of canonical privilege. Such an approach would be congenial and familiar to secular critics, who cannot in any case have a canon of absolute authority and fixity, and who tend to behave as if a loose notion of canonicity were an accurate reflection of the way things are, at any rate for the present, in professional circles. But it is perfectly plain, even from this proposal for compromise, that neither the Childs party nor the Barr party could accept it, for it violates theological and historiographic beliefs on both sides. It is moreover, much weaker magic: on the one hand it cannot make historical persons live again, or even show them as they were; and on the other it forfeits the advantages of that organic wholeness which is the concomitant of all doctrines of plenary inspiration. As a *via media* it simply won't do. Its rationality cannot compensate for the loss of magic.

Let me qualify the rather vague and possibly offensive term "magic." In *Wilhelm Meister* Goethe says *Hamlet* is like a tree, each part of it there for, and by means of, all the others. Five hundred years earlier a Kabalist said this of the Torah: "Just as a tree consists of branches and leaves, bark, sap and roots, each one of which components can be termed tree, there being no substantial difference between them, you will also find that the Torah contains many things, and all form a single Torah and a tree, without difference between them. . . . It is necessary to know that the whole is one unity." Thus Moses de Leon, perhaps the author of the main part of the Zohar, as quoted by Gershom Scholem.[6] Moses and Goethe seem to be saying very much the same kind of thing; certainly they have hit upon the same figure. We should be wrong, however, to make too much of the resemblance. The context of Goethe's remark is that of Romantic organicism and *Naturphilosophie*, of the philosophical and scientific proposals which interested him in his moment; and without some consideration of them as well as of more literary contexts we shall scarcely grasp the full quality of his saying about *Hamlet*. The beautiful excesses, if so we think them, of Kabbalistic commentary belong, despite the similarity of the figures, to a different world. One might get some measure of the difference by comparing the context provided for one by the scholarship of Scholem with that provided by the scholarship of M. H. Abrams toward the understanding of nineteenth century organicism. The idea of the work as organism is ancient and powerful, but we do not suppose that it serves exactly the same purpose whenever it recurs; it will have a difference enforced by its position within a contemporary structure of belief (though that is yet another if less definite holistic notion). Potent critical myths may sleep and be rediscovered, but they do not return to just the same place. The Kabbalah had its organicism, and so did Romantic thought; we have legacies from both, though the latter is still the one that is more continuous with our own presuppositions, which may explain why most of us would think the Kabbalah the more "magical" of the two.

It is worth dwelling for a moment on these differences. To the Kabbalist, and even to the Talmudist, the text may be said to be coextensive with the world, and coeval with it; it is indeed, like ritual, out of time. Thus it does not prevent the kinds of problem that scientific philology was invented to solve, any more than it needs to adapt an idealist philosophy. There are no redactions, no contradictions, no errors even, that cannot be explained or explained away in terms of the text itself; there is perfect unity and inexhaustible sense. The closure of the text is obviously of great importance, whatever historians may say of its fortuity; it stimulated and governed commentary, and the commentary became part of the world of the text, an Oral Torah that articulated what had been there, latent, from the creation. For Torah was present on that occasion, though Torah is also called midrash of Torah. The application of the sacred text to all later times is only a continuation of a process that began when everything began, so that there is no divorce between application and understanding; the meaning is the meaning of both the original and the latest accepted interpretation. The tradition is continuous, and however novel the explanations they were part of a transhistorical whole; Scholem says of the ideas of Isaac Luria that "for all their glaring novelty" they were "not regarded as a break with traditional authority."[7] It was Luria who thought of the Torah as having 600,000 faces, each turned to only one of the 600,000 at Sinai. The officially fixed text could indeed generate any number of interpretations; individual letters and their numerical values have secret senses, new insights arise from the alteration of vowels within the consonantal stems; ever conceivable device may be used to get at the white fire behind the black fire of the Torah. It is there to be read, but—wrapped in secrecy. Some say that the Israelites at Sinai heard only the first or the first two commandments before being awed into deafness by the divine voice, so that the rest were known only in the accommodated forms provided by Moses; or even that they heard only the first of God's word, "I," *anoki*, or perhaps only the first consonant, the *aleph*, so that the prophets continually explicate that hugely pregnant but silent consonant.[8] It is, to recall a line of Stevens, a world of words to the end of it; a world of written words, and of letters and the spaces between them.

Compared with all this, our way of talking about the world of a poem, or of the creative act of imagination—and in so far as we still do so we are harking back to Goethe—sounds self-consciously figurative and feeble. For here is the extremest and most magical form of application; the text becomes a type of its interpretations; it is prophetic of all futures and all readers, since in principle it contains them; its truth is concealed and revealed in words that constitute the world. The later organicism dealt in analogy rather than identity. Moreover, it grew up alongside the new historical philology, which was radically opposed to it. Out of that strife was born modern hermeneutics. As we have seen, the struggle continues; it is now a struggle between weaker, less confident varieties of magic, the canonical and the historical.

More precisely, it can be said that the new hermeneutics came into existence when historical criticism (begun as a secular activity and so not at the outset troubled by questions of faith) began to be applied to the scriptures. And each of them—history and hermeneutics, or by extension Barr and Childs—is the shadow of the other. The title of founder of modern hermeneutics is usually given to Schleiermacher, who was also a major New Testament historical critic. He believed in a universal hermeneutic but also said that "a continuing preoccupation with the New Testament canon which was not motivated by one's own interest in Christianity could only be directed against the canon."[9] This must mean that if you really treated it as you would any other ancient document you would be forced to dismantle it; therefore it must be given special treatment. The wish to resolve such difficulties gave rise to ever more subtle hermeneutic formulations, defences against the dismantling historian. It is not really possible to understand them outside that context. Dilthey was a pupil of Ranke. Heidegger took on the entire opposing tradition, and made the world hermeneutic. Yet to speak of the anti-objectivist hermeneutics in this way is to study them historically, as Gadamer does. One approach becomes the shadow of the other. Whenever we think about writing history we face problems that are best thought of hermeneutically; whenever we think of understanding and application, or of the developing notion of the hermeneutic circle, we are obliged to take account of history.

We cannot escape this double, nor should we wish to, wherever our sympathies lie in such disputes as that between Barr and Childs. It does seem that we have to recognise that all historical knowledge has to be understood with an understanding that includes not only the facts, the events and persons, but our own limited comprehension of them; and that we must see that those conditioned understandings themselves have a history which confirms that, like all understandings, they are likely to prove transient. This does not mean we should not believe and act upon our understandings, a point neatly made by D. C. Hoy in his book *the Critical Circle*[10]: the belief that my belief will be shown to be wrong does not invalidate my belief. The view that there are no eternal truths does not entail that there is no truth.

The revival or redevelopment of canonical criticism, remote as it is from the Jewish variety or indeed from that of the early Church, mild and concessive as it is, strenuously opposed as it is by the historian, seems to me to be a matter of more than local interest. It has some bearing upon secular literary criticism. I cannot at this late moment enter into this tricky and rather fashionable subject, but it may be worth saying this much. The great modernist critics (and authors; sometimes they were the same persons) were inclined to holism. Eliot, for instance, had quite a magical view of the literary canon, though he thoughtfully provided for the possibility of adding to it. The New Criticism believed at least in the autonomy of works of art and explored their latent internal relations. Opposition came from literary historians; or it might come from Marxists, or from all who believe that to confer upon some works the special status implied by their description as literature was false in itself. Deconstruction, perhaps oddly, has its canon, and to some practitioners it seems that only great works, which are great because they have already deconstructed themselves, are worth deconstructing. But whether some version of the canon is endorsed, or whether all canons are anathematized, we can detect in each of the combatants presuppositions, of which they may be largely unconscious. Their struggles are not unlike those of Childs and Barr, each side having to hear the other speak in order to complete its own argument; for example, orthodox literary history, thought by its practitioners to be the most natural and sensible thing in the world, has its own mythology of period, its own magical plot of history, regarded as beyond criticism. Finally, the argument between the theologians seems to illustrate a more general problem: history struggles with its hermeneutic shadow; hermeneutics with simple history. There is magic in both, and magic is no longer a powerful preservative, so that all we can be sure of is that the terms of the argument will change once again, and it will seem to no one that either party has laid a hand on what might be called the truth. At any rate, that is the truth as I happen to see it at the moment.

NOTES

1. W. G. Kümmel, *The New Testament: The History of the Investigation of Its Problems* (1973, from the German edition of 1970) pp. 304–305.
2. Kümmel, p. 373.
3. Hans-Georg Gadamer, *Truth and Method* (1975, from the German 2nd ed. of 1965; 1st ed., 1960), pp. 295–296.
4. Gadamer, p. 301.

5. Gadamer, pp. 307–309.
6. Gershom Scholem, *The Kabbalah and Its Symbolism* (1965, ed. of 1969, from the German ed. of 1960), p. 46.
7. Scholem, p. 21.
8. Scholem, p. 30.
9. Kümmel, p. 425.
10. D. C. Hoy, *The Critical Circle* (1978), p. 139.

The Gospels as Narrative

JAMES M. ROBINSON

The bulk of the New Testament consists of narrative. This has not been considered up until very recent times as of any particular relevance. Christian theology proceeded by and large to prefer the syllogism, or to debase the particular as but an instance at the bottom of the pyramid leading via species to genera and upward and onward to the universal, ultimately leading to being itself or to the Supreme Being.

With the rise of romanticism and historicism we did become more aware of biblical history as perhaps in some way significant as history or narrative in distinction from metaphysics. And yet the initial attempts to do anything about it were often such as to lead more sober minds to shy away, as in the case of a purported difference between the Jewish-Christian mentality as linear and temporal in an invidious contrast to the pagan mind as circular or spatial, or in the case of a "holy history" that is or should be exempt from the critical methods of secular historiography.

It is my hope, and the basis of my keen interest in the transactions of this symposium, that the heightened interest in narrative as a literary form on the part of literary critics over the past few years may provide a promising way for biblical scholarship to come to grips more effectively with the narrativity of much of the biblical text.

The narrative tradition of the Bible does not of course begin with the Gospels. Already in the tenth century before the Christian era Israel developed an oriental court where scribes both wrote down the cycles of oral legend that had accumulated among the tribes during the preceding centuries and wrote up the history of the rise to power of the Davidic dynasty during the preceding decades. Over the next half a millennium these two kinds of narrative were worked and reworked into the historical books of the Hebrew Bible, to be retold in Chronicles and Jubilees and supplemented in Maccabees and Josephus. With the final destruction of the temple and the resultant loss of identity it had provided, these narrative texts served in large part to solidify Judaism, right down to the modern state of Israel. Yet the Gospels as narrative cannot simply be derived from the Hebrew Bible or Jewish culture. The very absence of any biography of the anonymous founder of the Essenes, known to us only under the title of the Teacher of Righteousness, indicates that such a strong narrative tradition in no way necessitates the emergence of biographies of Jesus.

Nor is there anything in Jesus or primitive Christianity as such that would really make narrative Gospels unavoidable. Jesus told fictional short stories. Alongside these parables, miracle stories and pithy sayings embedded in a minimal narrative framework circulated orally among his followers as well as perhaps in small written collections. The passion narrative had an apologetic urgency largely met by proof from scripture. Yet the prominence of non-narrative forms of primitive Christian writing, such as the Pauline letters and the collection of largely disconnected sayings of Jesus we call Q, makes it clear that the emergence of the narrative Gospels is not to be taken as a matter of course. It must reflect special circumstances well worth our investigation, for what they imply both about primitive Christianity and about the Gospels themselves.

It is here that I would hope that literary criticism could provide biblical scholarship with perhaps decisive reconceptualizations and imaginative insights that would take the current status of biblical research, with its assured results but dreary categories, and recast the discipline into an exciting, informative and progressive area of research for the coming generation. I am myself still such a novice in recent literary criticism that I cannot here and now carry through such a promising venture, though it is in my view of sufficient moment that I would hope at some later juncture to provide a more mature statement.

The greatest threat to biblical scholarship in our time is the dearth of brilliant minds in the discipline, a situation no doubt resulting from our failure to reconceptualize what we are about in such a way as to challenge the best minds of our day. If the humanities as such are not to follow the demise of classics in our culture that we have lamented over the past century, we must devote ourselves primarily to reflecting on what we are really at and how we are to get at it, rather than simply to grinding out more data to assemble into outmoded and irrelevant categories. It is from such distinguished literary critics as those assembled here, as well as from the French connection of Yale and Johns Hopkins, that exciting new ways of thinking about texts and our relation to them have emerged.

In my presentation I do not propose to summarize what New Testament scholarship has done of late in dependence on such literary criticism, for example with regard to the parables, but rather to take the main line of recent research regarding the Gospels (which has been taking place largely in ignorance of literary criticism)—such things as the redaction criticism that has dominated the past generation of New Testament scholarship—and seek to begin the rethinking of its relatively assured results in ways that literary criticism might illuminate.

Christianity in the first century of the common era was endowed with a series of strong texts, with "precursors" a major problem with which "ephebes" had to cope. The changed situation that required Matthew and Luke to differ from Mark as widely as they did was in large part that Mark did not have to cope with Mark, whereas they did! If such "anxiety of influence" is evident at the end of the period of writing canonical Gospels, it may be conjectured to have been also present earlier in the trajectory, where the composition of Mark is to be located. Since redaction criticism has convinced us that Mark was not just a collector or editor, but a theologian and author of sorts, it is appropriate to ask what were the strong texts with which he or she may have had to come to terms and how did one cope with them?

Much of the difficulty in studying Mark has to do with the fact that it is the oldest extant Gospel, so that what lies behind it must to a considerable extent be hypothetical. For this reason the procedures one might envisage for discussing the difficult case of Mark and his precursors may be exemplified, practiced, in the later more discussable Gospels, before turning back to Mark itself.

Redaction criticism should have taught us to understand the Gospels in large part in terms of where they differed. One may illustrate from the Gospel of John. The last editor of the Fourth Gospel, the so-called ecclesiastical redactor, added a final chapter and various interpolations into the body of the all-too spiritual Gospel in order to aim it toward orthodoxy. Recognition of the difference between evangelist and editor marks a major insight into the positions of both texts: The orthodoxy of the Gospel of John that qualified it for canonicity is not original to the text itself. The orthodoxy of the text was introduced when the ecclesiastical redactor grappled with the strong text with which he or she had to cope, namely a dangerously spiritual Gospel. To move one step further back, the spiritual Evangelist in turn had interpolated or appended otherworldly meanings into the physical miracle stories of the Semeia Source that he or she was editing as one's strong text. Recognition of the difference between the meaning of the Semeia Source and that given to it in the spiritual Gospel is one of the most significant new insights in the study of Johannine theology. Thus, the ecclesiastical redactor, in order to correct the spiritual Evangelist's deviation and thus to bring the Gospel back into mainline Christianity, tended belatedly to undo the divergence from the Semeia Source that the spiritual Evangelist had carried out. This view, first implemented in the form of a commentary on John by Rudolf Bultmann, has gained increasing acceptance over the past generation.

This orthodox trend, that ultimately brought John into the canon alongside the other Gospels, had in the new canonical context the paradoxical effect of reasserting the relative spirituality of the Gospel of John. For, standing over against the Synoptic Gospels in the canonical context, John again seemed remarkably spiritual, in fact precisely now gaining the designation "spiritual Gospel," in spite of all the toning down by the ecclesiastical redactor that had first made such a comparison with the Synoptics in the canonical context possible.

Thus Johannine theology, understood as theology moving along this trajectory, can be aptly understood as a sequence of secondary meanings, as it moves from one set of distinctions to another along its trajectory, with its canonical meaning not present all along, but deferred until its canonization—a situation that clearly invites deconstruction, as older, suppressed layers of hidden meaning undermine the canonical meaning and in fact have served as a seedbed for future "heresy," as such secret meanings have tended to surface one after the other.

Similarly redaction criticism has taught us to understand Matthean and Lucan theology as meanings superimposed secondarily upon their source materials, especially the two identifiable texts they used, namely the Sayings Source we call Q and the Gospel of Mark. Matthew and Luke incorporated these sources, thereby acknowledging them as strong texts, but yet ignoring the difference between them by putting them in a check-and-balance system, the fusion of one with the other. Yet this elimination of the difference marked by the separate texts Q and Mark itself makes a big difference!

Redaction criticism has perhaps focussed its attention all too exclusively on the alteration of wording that the latter Evangelists effected here and there, leaving unresolved how to assess the fact that the later Evangelists did after all incorporate, quite literally accept, some ninety percent of their sources. Thus redaction criticism has not really known how to assess the traditional reading of the later Gospels, which has usually been harmonistic, treating them as hardly more than a reproduction of the earlier Gospels with but minor alterations, a view which of course cannot be contested on quantitative terms. But it can be contested in terms of the differences and hence the meanings they did and did not observe. With a flick of one's brush a painter can highlight a picture so as to give the whole a new cast.

Matthew and Luke not only approved of Q and Mark sufficiently to be able to incorporate them, but also disapproved of them not only in specific details but also in the sense of not observing the structural difference between them. Whatever made Q shy away from narrative and Mark shy away from sayings is a difference that has disappeared from Matthew and Luke, both of whom superimposed a new meaning on Q in the only way Q was accepted into the canon, namely imbedded in Matthew and Luke, and likewise superimposed a new meaning upon Mark as merged with Q in the harmonistic products of Matthew and Luke.

The canonizing process did it again to Mark, not by excluding it, as was the fate of Q, but by sandwiching it in between Matthew and Luke and hence ultimately degrading it into what was taken to be an abridgement of Matthew, to play a negligible role in the history of Christianity. Canonical Q, lost in Matthew and Luke and thus deprived of its difference from Mark, and canonical Mark, deprived of its difference from no-longer-existent Q, are by this very fact misreadings of the meanings these texts had when they were originally composed in quite eloquent differentiation from each other. What we encounter in the canon is a substitution of meanings in line with the ongoing canonizing process, which has of course preserved Q and Mark, but at the cost of having recast the meaning that was suggested by their structure, so that it played little or no role in the history of Christianity and has to be hypothesized by scholarly inquiry today.

Thus, in the trajectory leading to the canonical Gospels, the last quarter of the first century already superimposed meaning on Gospels which had come from the third quarter of the century, by eliminating the differences that gave those earlier Gospels their distinct profiles and thus their meanings. Perhaps these earlier meanings of the Gospels were in turn meanings superimposed on the tradition behind them. The present paper is concerned with this deferral of meaning at each successive stage in the trajectory from oral tradition to Q and Mark and beyond, in order to locate Mark in a sequence and thus to define its meaning, its political posture, as a first tentative step toward making use of some of the insights of literary criticism to elucidate crucial transactions in the narrative tradition of the New Testament. Hence we now turn to the Gospel of Mark, its oral or written precursors, and how it was shaped by them as it made its own statement.

The Gospel of Mark in the Vulgate translation used in the Middle Ages and in the King James translation used in English literature concludes with resurrection appearances that were belatedly added to the Gospel to obscure its difference both from the later canonical Gospels and in a quite different sense from the earlier pre-Markan tradition as well. Why did Mark include no resurrection appearances? Perhaps because such narratives of appearances as were available were not acceptable, due to secondary meanings that had come to be associated with them. For they presented the resurrected Jesus as luminous, such as the blinding light Acts depicts at Paul's conversion on the Damascus road. Admittedly we are most familiar with this kind of resurrection appearance not from the canon but from later Gnostic Gospels, where the resurrected Christ appears liberated from the shackles of the flesh in the glory of a luminous heavenly body or bodilessness, teaching esoteric Gnostic truth, in a narrative framework of disembodied apparitions, to the clique that uses such dialogues to validate its own off-beat variety of Christianity.

This may be the reason why the narration of the appearance to Peter, listed as first and hence as basic by Paul and Luke (1 Cor. 15:5; Lk. 24:34), but, oddly enough, not narrated at the end of any of the Gospels, got lost—except in an apocryphal Gospel of Peter, where it is one of these Gnostic-like luminous apparitions! The Gospel of Mark may have been aware of and felt compelled to pay at least lip service to this dangerously luminous resurrection appearance to Peter, in that it may have been too authoritative to be completely omitted. For the author of Mark would seem to have put it back into the middle of the public ministry, thereby tying it down to earthy bodiliness, as the narrative we call the transfiguration story (Mk. 9:2–8). In this way the luminous resurrection appearance was integrated into the public ministry, rather than outtrumping it.

This displacement of the luminous apparition to Peter, collapsing the difference between the earthly Jesus and the resurrected Lord that the luminous apparition implied, can be compared to Luke's procedure regarding the luminous apparition to Paul. Luke also sensed the heretical meaning such luminous narratives were coming to imply in his time, and hence created a periodizing difference between the resurrected Jesus, whose presence was limited to forty days, and the church guided by the Holy Spirit in the absence of the resurrected. This periodization was carried out specifically for the purpose of playing down the older difference between the earthly Jesus and the resurrected Lord.

Paul was the victim of this political move on Luke's part, in that Paul was demoted from eyewitness to the resurrection and hence apostle, to the lesser role of hero of the book of Acts. Thus Luke put the appearance to Paul of the resurrected Lord, now demoted into Paul's conversion experience, many chapters later (Acts 9) than the normative period of resurrection appearances (Lk. 24; Acts 1). Paul's conversion becomes only a significant moment within church history, with an invidious meaning of inferiority to the "twelve" as the original apostles, a distinction that had been strongly opposed by Paul (Ga. 1:1.12), was advocated by his opponents during his lifetime (1 Cor. 9:2), and is now granted canonical status in Acts. Thanks to the aggressive politics carried out by Luke, valid appearances were henceforth characterized in orthodox circles not so much by their difference from Jesus' public ministry as by their difference from religious experience within church history.

What was wrong with the luminous appearances was not only their inadequacy to mark the difference from ghostlike unreal visionary experiences and thus their insufficiency to affirm the literal physical reality of the resurrection, but also their remarkable adequacy to mark the difference of the resurrected Lord from the traditions of the earth-bound Jesus associated with his public ministry. What the resurrected Lord taught, after having been freed of bodily limitations and having gone to heaven, was clearly presented as a higher truth, an ultimate revelation. This would have functioned as an invidious comparison with the groping sayings and earth-bound stories of Jesus of Nazareth with which main-line Christianity sought to validate its claim to apostolicity and canonical authority. Paul himself intentionally ignores Jesus "according to the flesh," since all has become new (2 Cor. 5:16–17). When in the grip of a Gnosticizing trajectory, Jesus of Nazareth risked the same fate as orthodoxy accorded to John the Baptist, of becoming associated with the old dispensation as no more than its culmination and flowering, on the wrong side of a dividing line that made all the difference. That is to say, the resurrected Lord is set over against Jesus of Nazareth as the spiritual over against the literal, the *sensus plenior* over against the *sensus litteralis*, as the New Testament over against the Old Testament. Indeed this Gnosticizing trace sensed in the resurrected Lord may have been the first germ of the idea of a New Testament, just as a century later the "heretic" Marcion produced the first implementation of the idea of a New Testament in the form of a collection of texts.

A pair of antithetic terms came to mark the difference between the lower and the higher level of revelation, the terms "in riddles" versus "in openness," or, as we are accustomed to it in the King James idiom, "in parables" versus "openly" in Mark (3:23; 4:11; 8:25.32), and "in proverbs" versus "plainly" in John (16:25.29). When both Mark and John, apparently independently of each other, shift the point at which one turned from the lower level to the higher level back from Easter to a point prior to the passion, they are intentionally relocating the cleft that gave emergent Christian Gnosticism its opening. Thus narrative (in the form of Mark and John) was introduced into the New Testament not simply because of a narrational mind-set of biblical religion or the like, but rather as a proto-orthodox misreading of a traditional difference between Jesus and the resurrected Lord that was becoming increasingly unacceptable to main-line Christianity.

The Fourth Gospel seems to have done much the same thing as did Mark, yet without dependence in this regard upon Mark—it is as if they were responding to an analogous situation in the morphology of primitive Christianity, as new meanings came to be associated with the older texts and traditions, thus necessitating a restructuring. This convergence between Mark and John without dependence one upon the other is strikingly analogous in this regard to that between Matthew and Luke, who also were not dependent the one on the other, and yet each one did very much the same thing as the other, in merging Mark and Q. It is as if the Evangelists cannot really be understood on the basis of the private creativity of individual authors in the traditional sense, but more appropriately to be understood as the products of overarching shared social forces, the main ones really clear to us being their literary precursors.

This sociological dimension of even the first, pre-literary generation of Christianity has been illuminated especially under the now-familiar rubric of the "itinerant radicalism" of first-generation prophets continuing the ministries of John the Baptist and Jesus in Palestine. The texts of the New Testament are products of Diaspora Christianity, literacy, Greek hegemony, the cosmopolitanism of Antioch, Ephesus, Corinth and the like. The pre-literary Jesus movement took place in the native hamlets of Galilee, among predominantly Aramaic-speaking peasants and fisherfolk, largely illiterate and poverty-struck, ultimately dependent on Diaspora cosmopolitan Christianity for their fate, at first a dole (the collections made by Paul in the Diaspora on their behalf), and finally an atavistic status as the shrivelling heresy of Ebionitism that gradually faded from the pages of history. Originally these itinerant radicals had renounced home, family, possessions and protection, a life style that ultimately was tolerated in mainline Christianity only as the exceptional status of monasticism, an ideal to be honored but not enforced on the church at large. For the cosmopolitan church opted for a charitable patriarchalism where middle-class virtues such as the Christian home replaced the intolerable and futureless celibate radicalism of Jesus and his followers.

In the case of the Old Testament, narrative literature presupposed the transition from the time of the judges, when everyone was a law unto oneself, into the time of the monarchy, when court life made it possible for sources of the Pentateuch to be recorded and the history of the Davidic dynasty to be produced. Just so the emergence of the Gospels has to do with the transition from the barefooted, pennyless, unlettered, mendicant, transient native to the moderately educated, literate, sedentary, cosmopolitan, hellenized Evangelist. It is another of the ironies of the canonizing process that this difference between Jesus, his family and followers on the one hand, and the Evangelists and their Greek church on the other, was completely obscured by the claim of the canonizers to represent apostolic Christianity. They accredited themselves by claiming to have Gospels composed by (or under the direct authority of) the very Jesus people whose position the Evangelists had usurped to make Christianity safe and guarantee it a future. One cannot but recall the ambivalence of the term *traditio*, the "handing over" of the past both in the sense of its transmission and its betrayal.

The recent study of early Christian prophets as the reproclaimers of Jesus' sayings has further clarified what is at work in the interaction of the Q tradition of Jesus' sayings and the narrative Gospels. To judge by Q, early Christian prophets did not proclaim the death and resurrection of Jesus as saving events, as does the New Testament—both Paul and the Gospels—but rather reflected "Easter faith" in the (to-us) novel form, it may well have been the earlier form, of assuming that Jesus' sayings had no more been invalidated by his death than had John the Baptist's drastic warning of imminent doom been invalidated for Jesus by the Baptist's death. The sayings themselves were what had in effect survived beheading and crucifixion and were alive and active in the hamlets of Galilee. Without mention of the twelve, the apostles, churches, or even Christians (much less bishops, apostolic succession, and the like), the Jesus people continued proclaiming what Jesus had said. They differed primarily only in that they took their inspiration from him and so ascribed to him their sayings, repeating sayings they recalled him having said, adapted to their present needs, and formulating new sayings that they presented not only with their own authority, but rather in his name. But this implicit christology was not oriented to Jesus as a figure of the past, but rather to eternal divine Wisdom, that had spoken through John the Baptist and Jesus, but now continued as the resurrected Lord to speak through the early Christian prophets, an implicit christology that made it possible for them to identify the resurrected Lord with the judge of the end of time, the Son of Man.

We catch sight of this early Christian prophecy primarily in Q, whose ambivalent status as a non-surviving text may be symbolically appropriate as a witness to an oral phenomenon that Christianity intentionally buried in Matthew and Luke. For the prophets' constant updating of the Jesus tradition ultimately gave priority to its present reformulation over its traditional formulation, and thus led further and further away from Jesus, as ever-changing responses kept the tradition in flux. It may well be that the almost exclusive focus of Q on disconnected unprotected sayings is a function of this ever-changing openness of the sayings tradition to the present situation. For the slight narrative framework of a pronouncement story and the narration of miracle stories, in spite of their contemporary relevance of advocating an idea or promoting a cure, none-theless do so in the stabilizing refraction of a flash-back to a past setting or a past occurrence. The final writing down of Q itself reflects some of this narrative tendency, in that Q, though basically just a chain of disconnected sayings, does begin in a quasi-narrative way with sayings of the precursor John the Baptist and then Jesus' dialogue with Satan at the temptation.

When one returns to Mark, the difference between Mark and Q is nevertheless striking: Mark is notorious for its relative lack of sayings of Jesus, in spite of its abstract emphasis on Jesus teaching. This lack would seem to be Mark's way of eliminating the authority of early Christian prophets and the theology they implied. After all, early Christian prophets are mentioned by Mark only as an abomination of the end time, when "many will come in my name, saying, 'I am he!' and they will lead many astray. . . . And then if any one says to you, 'Look, here is the Christ!' or 'Look, there he is!' do not believe it. False Christs and false prophets will arise and show signs and wonders, to lead astray, if possible, the elect. But take heed; I have told you all things beforehand" (Mk. 13:6, 21–23). Mark repudiates the prophets in order to validate the older layer of traditions, by locating these traditions emphatically prior to Easter, where for him authority is based, letting the resurrected Lord literally say nothing. To be sure, Mark writes for the present, and thus stands close enough to the ethos of the early Christian prophets to narrate the past in a way transparent to the present. Mark is in fact a transitional text between orality and textuality. But whereas Q stands nearer orality, Mark stands nearer textuality.

This Marcan refraction of Jesus traditions into the present is a phenomenon no longer characteristic of Luke, who marks the difference between the present and the past with a periodizing procedure that makes of Jesus' ministry a paradisaical island in the middle of flux, a haven of refuge, a golden age, where the pure ideal makes sense in that the power of the devil is for a time suspended. But Jesus himself (according to Lk. 22:31–38) called this ideal life style to a halt at the beginning of the passion narrative. One may recall that it is the same Luke who, in the book of Acts, can idealize a communal life style in the original Jerusalem church without jeopardizing the more bourgeois life style of Luke's own time. Thus

Luke does not need to update Q constantly to a state his own life style can actualize, but, much to the relief of New Testament scholarship, left Q much as it was, to let the cat out of the bag as to the itinerant radicalism, the nonviolent peasant revolt, with which it all began.

The addition of the book of Acts to the Gospel is itself a function of the shift taking place as one moves from Mark to Luke: If Mark could retain the double refraction of preserving the tradition while addressing the present, Luke here makes a distinction, the price he has to pay for insuring the integrity of the past more than had Mark. If the past receives from Luke the security and protection that a museum provides, it inevitably must be supplemented by some separate updating. Thus the Gospel becomes a sort of Old Testament to which the Book of Acts is the New Testament, a quite new and revolutionary difference. If by pushing back Q completely out of contemporaneity Luke was able to save its wording more nearly intact, he did this at the price of erasing from history early Christian prophecy as the reproclaiming of Jesus' sayings. According to the loaded construct in Acts, Jesus continued to speak only forty days after the crucifixion, then ascended to heaven to be represented, after a dead silence of ten days, by the Holy Spirit, with the early Christian prophets of Galilee who had reproclaimed Jesus' sayings, indeed with Galilean Christianity as a whole, carefully overlooked: "in Jerusalem and in all Judea and Samaria and to the end of the earth" (Acts 1:8).

The transition from the pre-Gospel traditions to the Gospel of Mark can also be approached in terms of the shift from orality to textuality, as has been proposed by Werner H. Kelber (*The Oral and the Written Gospel*, 1983), who makes use of that pre-Derrida strand of literary criticism that privileges orality. He emphasizes the view that orality, still dominantly characteristic of Q, preserves "the presence of the living Lord" in a way basically terminated by the Gospel of Mark, who in effect silenced the living voice of Jesus and thereby finally put him to rest. Mark did not make use of the quantity of oral sayings that must have been available to him, precisely because of the need he sensed to terminate the immediacy and presence which orality reflected. By making full use of textuality, emphasizing traditions such as miracle stories and parables where presence is not so direct, Mark, who of necessity worked from oral traditions, nonetheless superimposed the ethos of textuality on the tradition. It is perhaps as part of this effort that one can sense a decided repudiation in Mark of the bearers of oral tradition, both the disciples and the family, an invidiousness or pointedness that is smoothed out by subsequent evangelists. Mark produces an objectifiable artifact, surrenders the control that orality maintains over the process of interpretation, and thus, by writing, functions intentionally as an outsider to the oral tradition. Matthew and Luke, once Mark has done its work and given them a written narrative with its distance and indirect communication as their frame of reference, could, without the risk Mark would have run, proceed to incorporate the written Q materials without fear of the problems of orality.

If the Fourth Gospel spoke for all subsequent Christians in pronouncing a blessing on those who do not see and yet believe, Mark vindicated the privileged position of posterity for not having heard and yet having understood. The oral transmittors could well have the sense of the immediate presence of the living Lord, an authoritatively and effectively mediated communication to the hearer, but his may have threatened Mark as the kind of "over-realized eschatology" that has also been identified (though in other categories) in the Pauline world. "The oral metaphysics of presence" was in Kelber's view disconfirmed by persecution and the Jewish war against the Romans around 70, and thereby shown to be fallacious, a crisis the Gospel of Mark by its very textuality seeks to overcome. The power of the Galilean Jesus movement, the first generation of actual disciples, is broken by Greek-speaking, literate, Diaspora Christianity of the second generation.

The Gospel of Mark is not only a passion narrative with a long introduction, as it has been defined for almost a century, but is itself as narrative the death of the Galilean public ministry that extended until about 70 C.E., bringing to a final termination the afterlife of the living Jesus speaking through prophets he inspired. The period around 70 C.E., is in many regards a turning point, with the suppression of the Jewish revolt through a prolonged war, the dying out of the first generation, the shift of the Christian population center out of Palestine and Judaism into the Diaspora and the Gentile world, the emergence of Gnosticism as an alluring-repelling new posture, and, perhaps, to an extent we have not traditionally recognized, the introduction of narrative texts, a political act of immeasurable significance down to the present day.

The implicit privileging of orality in these comments setting Mark over against Q may call for some corrective in terms of Derrida's relativizing of the distinction between orality and textuality by regarding orality as proto-writing, or, in terms of New Testament scholarship, the sense in which Q leads not only to the historical Jesus behind it but forward to Gnosticism ahead of it, such as the Gospel of Thomas. If part of the problem with Gnostics is that they were too full of themselves, holier than thou, religious snobs, know-it-alls, this metaphysics of presence with all its less-than-desirable overtones may be something it inherited from the wandering radicalism of Galilean Christianity. Is the claim of such charismatic prophets to be proclaiming the orality of the living Jesus itself really transmitting Jesus, or is it betraying Jesus?

Jesus proclaimed the imminent but still future kingdom, and the Galilean prophets proclaimed the presence of the resurrected Lord in their words. The presence of divine Wisdom in effect became the substitute for the delayed parousia, which thus brings us to the role of the supplement in Derridean deconstruction. If Jesus lost himself in his message of the still future ideal that left the present in a void, the metaphysics of presence inherent in the prophets reproclaiming Jesus' words as the fullness of the resurrected Lord's presence filled that void. Can one legitimately do this? Do not the very sayings of Jesus about the kingdom as future transmitted by the Q community undermine that metaphysics of presence? Does not this inner contradiction suggest a deconstruction as more loyal to the sayings of Jesus? If for him the idiom "kingdom of God" meant primarily the non-presence of God in the institutions of society that basked in a metaphysics of presence, is he being well served by a Christian metaphysics of presence in which the real presence of Christ in the eucharist, the preached word, the established church, Christendom, has blunted his devastating criticism of the metaphysical complacency of his day and ours?

These observations have sought to reproduce important segments of the present status of New Testament scholarship familiar to those in the trade in language that seeks a dialogue with the literary criticism that has been of late such an exciting area in the humanities here and abroad. It is to be hoped that this dialogue will continue and prove to be a broadening and revitalizing influence on New Testament studies and perhaps in literary criticism itself.

John Come Lately: The Belated Evangelist

DONALD FOSTER

The writer of the Gospel of John (whom I'll simply call "John") is
disquieted by his belatedness, by the fact that he comes after
Matthew, Mark, and Luke (to say nothing of Q), yet wishes to write
an authoritative account of Jesus' life. His motto is the Lord's
motto: "I am the door of the sheep. All who came before me were
thieves and robbers" (10:8). There were, of course, many before
John, as before Luke, who undertook "to compile a narrative" of
Jesus' life (Lk. 1:1); but none of them, if we may believe John,
succeeded. As we shall see, John's purpose is not to add one more to
a growing heap of apocryphal Gospels, nor even to write a supplement to the synoptics, but rather to provide the world—for the first
time, if belatedly—with the true Gospel of Jesus Christ. John
wishes to clarify the message of a badly misunderstood Son of God.
And in the process, he does more than a little campaigning on his
own behalf as belated evangelist.

From prologue to benediction, John's preoccupation with his late
arrival to the evangelistic field has a profound effect on the shape of
his narrative, for Jesus is presented throughout as the one who came
late and yet remained prior in time, place, and truth. First comes the
problem of the Baptist's priority. In his own lifetime, the Baptist
had a much greater following than Jesus; but we read in John's

Gospel that his sole purpose was to bear witness to his successor. "This was he," confesses John, "of whom I said, 'He who comes after me is *before* me'"—(*emprosthen*, prior in both time and place)—"'for he was [and always has been] *before* me'", (*prōtos*, again, prior in both time and place, emphatically so); and it is worth noting that John's tribute is repeated fifteen verses later, but with the first "was" (*ēn*) transformed to an "is" (*estin*), thus illustrating the evangelist's point that Jesus as Logos is the pre-existent victor over the "it was" of time (1:15,30). Only the Father and the Son can say, "*I am.*" John, when asked if he is the Christ or Elijah, or "the prophet" expected to precede the Christ, must confess, "I am not" (1:21). The Baptist, unlike Christ, is not eternally present. His disciples are required rather to turn and *follow* the shepherding Lamb of God (1:29–40).

This theme is continued in John's typically allegorical fashion in his account of the wedding feast at Cana. The old wine (the word of the prophets) gives out, followed by the water (the Baptist's ministry) which fills the stone jars (even as the Baptist completed the old dispensation of Law). Jesus than turns the water into new wine by the transforming power of the word. Much is made of the fact that the Lord's wine came last and yet is better than all that preceded it: "Every man sets forth the good wine first, and the worse when they are become drunk. You have kept the good wine until now" (2:10). Nevertheless, his mother Mary (like Israel) must be rebuked for urging him to act before the appointed hour.

When Jesus arrives in Sychar and sits beside the well of Jacob, it is already midday. In John's trope for Israel and the prophets, Jesus greets there a Samaritan who has had five men, the most recent of whom belongs to another woman. Jesus, the spiritual bridegroom, comes to her at the sixth hour, and after she has provided him with water, reveals to her the true worship of God, worship "in spirit and in truth." The woman then asks, "Are you superior to Jacob our father, who gave us the well, and drank from it himself, and his sons, and his cattle?" (4:12). The answer, of course, is yes—and the water which Jesus belatedly brings will not be drunk by *cattle*. "I know," says the woman, "that the Messiah is coming (he who is called Christ); when he comes, he will declare to us all things."

Answers Jesus, *egō eimi*—"I am he," or (more literally), "*I am*" (4:225–26).

Some days later, in the evening hours, Jesus's disciples depart before him across the lake. Darkness settles over the land, but Jesus does not come. The sea rises, as a great tempest begins to blow. Still he does not come. When at last he appears, he comes to them walking on the waves, saying, *egō eimi*—"It is I," or "*I am*" (6:20). And despite his belated appearance, Jesus proves that he has full command over the arrival of his antecedents; they arrive at their destination only with his miraculous, if belated, assistance.

His brothers precede him to the autumnal Feast of Tabernacles. All the Jews then look for him, saying, "Where is he?" (7:11), but Jesus' predecessors are no help in finding him. When at last he arrives, with the feast half-over, the people marvel that he knows the Law without having had to be taught by another. "You will seek me," he tells the Jews, "and you will not find me: you cannot come where *I am*" (7:34). Then, "on the *last* day of the feast, the *great* day, Jesus stood up and cried out, saying, 'if anyone thirst, let him come to me, and drink'" (7:37).

At still another feast, again on the last day of the week, Jesus comes to the five crowded porticoes of the Pool of Bethzatha where there lies "a multitude of weak, blind, crippled, withered," and other unfortunates, patiently waiting for the angel of God—for once a year or so, an apparently whimsical angel would stir the water, and watch as the cripples and blindmen made a mad scramble for the pool; he then healed the first one in. Jesus, in surveying this woeful sight, finds there a man who has been lying at poolside for thirty-eight years. Jesus asks him if he would like to be made whole. "Lord," the invalid replies, "I haven't a man to put me into the pool when the water is disturbed—and while I am coming, *another gets in before me*" (5:7). The poor fellow, needless to say, has an intense awareness of his inability to come first. But Jesus redeems him, saying, "Rise, take up your pallet, and walk" (5:8). Moreover, unlike the earlier incidents, water (i.e., the Baptist's ministry) is no longer a prerequisite for Jesus to perform his marvels—thereby illustrating John's words that "He must increase, but I must decrease" (3:30).

Once again in chapter nine—on the last day of the week as the night is approaching—Jesus heals a man, this time one who has been blind from the beginning, that is, from birth. The man's childhood prayers are answered at last when Jesus appears as the Logos which lightens the darkness, anointing his eyes with clay even as the Logos once fashioned father Adam out of clay. He then *sends* the man to wash in the Pool of Siloam, another figure for baptism. The order is chronologically reversed: one comes to the light through the word; baptism follows as the external sign of an inward grace already applied. And "the Jews hounded Jesus because he did such things *on the seventh day*" (5:16).

When Lazarus is ill, the Lord again arrives late. "When Jesus came, he found that Lazarus had already been in the tomb four days" (11:17). First Martha, then Mary, gently upbraids him for not having come sooner. "Lord," they tell him, "if you had been here, my brother would not have died"—but by this time, to quote the authorized Version, "he stinketh" (11:21, 32, 39). No matter. Jesus proves his transcendence over time and time's laws by raising his friend from the dead, with the result that a great multitude of people become his followers. The Pharisees, meanwhile, with a touch of unwitting irony, turn to one another and sigh, "You see that it's no use. Look, the world is coming *after* him"—*ho kosmos opisō autou apēlthen anōthen* (12:19).

The Jews, however, refuse to come after him. As noted by C. K. Barrett and others, John always makes a distinction between the "crowd," some of whom, at least, are willing to follow Jesus, and the "Jews," who continually resist him, supposing that their fathers Abraham, Jacob, and Moses, having come first, are greater than he. These Jewish pretensions to a prior sonship are emblematized by various individuals: for example, Nicodemus ("victor over the people") cannot at first comprehend the concept of being "born from above" or "born from before" (Gk. *anōthen*).[1] He does not perceive that Jesus, who comes *from above*, is able to beget sons *from above*, without relying on the prior seed of Abraham and Moses (3:3, 7, 31). Judas ("Judah") and Barabbas ("son of the father") are likewise Jews and would-be sons. Neither name originated with John, but he fits them neatly into his scheme of things by adding that Judas was a *thief*, not just a traitor, and Barabbas was not an insurrectionist as in the synoptics, but a *robber* (7:6; 18:40). Both men are thus identified as a figure for the Jews, those stubborn people who presume to have come before the Son. Judas and Barabbas are two of a kind: like all Jews in John's book, they are "sons of [their] father the devil."

Refusing to acknowledge the absolute preeminence of Jesus, the Jews are offended by the Lord's "I am" and outraged when he produces "signs" on the seventh day, when no work is to be done. They have no room in their hearts for a belated Son of God, for the "truth" is something revealed a long time ago to their fathers, to Abraham, Moses, and the prophets. But while the Jews continually look to supposed authorities whose hour came—and went—in ages past, Jesus stresses that his "hour has not yet come." This does not mean that he is less than Moses or Abraham—for where the Jews have been, he preceded them, and where he goes, they cannot follow—but he is, nevertheless, not to be fully manifested until the hour is late (2:4; 7:30; 8:20). It is not until the *Greeks* begin to seek him that he finally says, "Now is the hour come for the Son of Man to be glorified. . . . If anyone serves me, he must *follow* me" (12:23–26). And a voice from above confirms it.

In Gethsemane, when the Jews come to arrest Jesus, with the thief Judas leading the way, the Lord stops them with two words: *egō eimi*—"*I am*" (not, as in most English versions, "I am he," though again, it includes that meaning). Jesus is eternally present. The first time he tried out his "I am" on the Jews ("Before Abraham was, *I am*"), they took up stones to stone him (8:58–59). But this time, literally translated, they "went away *into the after* and fell on the earth" (*apēlthen eis ta opisō; opisō*, like *emprosthen*, is both temporal and spatial, denoting the *place of the follower* and the *time not yet arrived*—18:6). One thing that these thieves and robbers will not be able to take from Jesus is his everlasting preeminence.

But given all this, how does *Jesus'* victory over belatedness in any way solve *John's* problem? For John, too, arrives belatedly, following in the tracks of Q, Mark, Luke, Matthew, and a score of others. The answer is that John presents Jesus as the only begotten, if belated, Son of the Father, and himself in turn as the only true son of the Son. Adoptive sonship is open to everyone (1:12–13); but John's glory, like that of the Logos, is "glory as of the only begotten of the

Father, full of grace and truth" (1:14). At the last supper, for example, only one apostle lies in the bosom of the Son (13:23), even as the Son is the only one ever to lie in the bosom of the Father (1:18). Again at the crucifixion, only one disciple is honored as spiritual son: "When Jesus saw [his] mother and [the] disciple whom he loved standing near, he said to the mother, 'Woman, behold your son!' Then said he to the disciple, 'Behold, your mother!' And from that hour the disciple took her unto his own" (19:26–27).

But may we, then, safely identify John the evangelist as "the disciple whom Jesus loved"? The answer is both yes and no, for John's Gospel is mediated by still another father, that is, John the apostle, the disciple with whom the "Johannine" school or cult identified itself. Throughout John's Gospel, there moves a mysterious figure without a name who is always at the center of the action. He is denoted always by a circumlocutionary phrase, and he stands for Johannine, as opposed to Petrine, Christianity. For example, after Jesus' arrest, it is this nameless Johannine apostle, not Simon Peter as in the synoptics, who follows Jesus into the courtyard of the High Priest. Peter follows at a safe distance and remains outside until the nameless disciple comes to the door and lets him in—for *he* is now the door of the sheep in Jesus' stead. But Peter's belated arrival proves a disaster. When he finally enters in, he betrays Jesus with his words, saying, "I am not" (18:17ff.). He means, in each instance, "I am not Jesus' disciple," but his words stand in deliberate contrast with the "I am" of Jesus (and of John). The implication is that Peter and Petrine Christianity are not eternally present, but are negated by time.

After the resurrection, these two disciples are contrasted again. The Johannine disciple runs ahead and comes to the tomb, but waits discreetly outside. "Then Simon Peter came, following him, and entered into the tomb"—but he fails to understand. When the Johannine disciple enters, he sees, and believes (20:3–8). The two disciples then go their separate ways, each to his own home (20:10). There is a nice symmetry in these two stories: while Jesus was yet on earth, it was the representative of Johannine Christianity who was closest to him, with Peter as a confused and unreliable follower. After Jesus returned to the higher world, Peter was first to enter the place where the Son had been, and John followed. Even then, John, the faster runner, could easily have preempted him, but it was foreordained that the latter should enter in first and misconceive the truth, that the truth might be revealed instead to John, when his hour was come. Jesus once warned Peter that this would be so, though his words have not often been fully understood: "Where I am going," said the Lord to Simon, "you cannot follow me now; but you shall follow me *at the last*" (Gk. *husteron*—8:36), that is, after John shows him the way.

John undercuts Peter in other ways: Contrary to the synoptics, we read here that it was Andrew and *the Johannine disciple*, not Andrew and Peter, who were the first to follow Jesus. Peter came in third. And when Simon at last appears, Jesus calls him "*Kēphas*," John's transliteration of the Aramaic, which, as he explains, means *Petros*, or "rock," but which to a Greek reader would have looked like *Kēphēn*, a "drone," "literary plagiarist," or "worn-out, decrepit person" (Scott and Liddell). Matthew, Mark, and Luke generously omit the transliteration. Moreover, the evangelist moves Peter's home from Capernaum to Bethsaida, on the far side of the lake from the village identified with Jesus, while moving the home of the Johannine apostle to Jerusalem, the city of God and of the glorified Christ. No longer is Peter the foundation of the Church, with the keys to heaven and hell in his right hand. He is instead a rather thick-headed Jew who sees the Son without perceiving, hears the message but does not understand. John likens him to those faithless Jews who asked scornfully of Jesus, "Where is this fellow ready to go that we shall not find him? Is he ready to go to the Greek dispersion and teach the *Greeks*? What is this logos which he speaks?" (7:35–36; cf. 8:36–37).

Simon Peter and Jesus do not seem to speak the same language. In John's version of the last supper, for example, the Lord's sacrament of foot-washing utterly bewilders him; and when he wishes to know which disciple is the traitor, Peter cannot ask Jesus himself, but must defer to the Lord's beloved. If Peter is to know the truth, it must be mediated by John. Again, in John's account of Gethsemane, it is Simon Peter, and not just "one of those who stood by" (Mk. 14:47), who misunderstands, draws his sword, and strikes off a man's ear. John gives the victim a name—Malchus, from the

Aramaic for "King." Peter, in resisting the Lord's Passion, has rashly injured a symbolic substitute for the Lord himself, who is, paradoxically, both King and slave of the High Priest.

John undermines Peter even in his nomenclature: John prefers to call him *Simon* Peter, and stresses that he is *the son of Jonah*, Jonah being the prophet described always in early Christian literature as the one who sinfully resisted God's will in bringing the true religion to the Gentiles; and "son of" always implies in John, as in Hebrew scripture, a likeness, a following-in-the-footsteps-of. Peter is like Jonah in perceiving Christianity as a religion of and for the Jews. And John gives a patronym to Judas Iscariot. He is now Judas Iscariot, *the son of Simon*. Except in Gethsemane, John never mentions Judas without calling him the son of Simon. This does not mean that John wants us to think of Judas as the biological son of Simon, but he is certainly driving home the likeness of the two disciples who betrayed the Logos, the Son of God, with false words.

It may seem odd at first that the Johannine disciple should go nameless while these other men's names receive such detailed attention—but in order for John the evangelist to take his place as the true son, *the name of the intervening father must be effaced*. The name "John" is used here only in reference to John the Baptist—who in turn is never called "John the Baptist," or "the Baptist," but simply "John." In his typically symbolic fashion, John thus takes from the beloved apostle his birthright as the spiritual son, effacing the name of that apostle so that he, John, may assume his rightful place as the disciple whom Jesus loved, tracing his genealogy directly from Father, to Son, to himself as belated evangelist. John's relation to the son of Zebedee is precisely that of Jesus to the Baptist: one is the true son, the only begotten of the father, while the other is a mere herald, who bears witness to the light but is not that light. We may therefore hear, in chapter 5, for example, the two sons, Jesus and John, speaking in unison:

> You sent to John [the Baptist and the Apostle], and he has born witness to the truth. Not that the testimony which I receive is from man; but I say these things that you may be saved. That man was a burning and visible lamp, and for a season you were willing to rejoice in his light. But the testimony which I have is superior

to that of John, for the works which my Father has granted me to make complete, these very works which I produce, bear me witness that the Father has sent me. And the Father who sent me has himself borne witness to me. (5:33–37)

John the apostle, like John the Baptist, is unworthy even to loosen the sandal-thong of the one coming after him, for "John produced no sign" (or, "no written proof," Gk. *sēmeion*—10:41). It is a commonplace of criticism to note that Jesus and John speak so much alike that it is impossible to tell where each speaker begins and ends. No two versions have the quotation marks in the same places; the above is one of many passages in which the speaker is not just Jesus or John, but both at once; here, as so often, John finds his words freighted with a double burden of truth.

The evangelist intuits that he is skating on thin ice in suggesting that his testimony is superior to that of his mentor, John the apostle, for if the gospel was not actually dictated to him by an eyewitness, what authority does it have? John insists, therefore, that his gospel is based on the apostle's firsthand experience—"He who saw it has borne witness; his testimony is true, and he knows that he speaks truly, that you also may believe" (19:35)—but in his narrative John goes far beyond anything the apostle could have told him, and he frequently contradicts the synoptics. How, then, can anyone be sure that his gospel is true? This problem of authority is the same one faced by the belated Son of man, who says, "If I bear witness to myself, then my testimony is not true. There is another [John] who bears witness to me" (5:31–32); later, though, when the Jews seem to trap him, saying, Aha! here you are, bearing witness to yourself, he replies, "Well, even if I *do* bear witness to myself, my testimony is true, for I know whence I have come. . . . I bear witness to myself, and the Father who sent me bears witness to me" (8:13–18).

That John bears witness to himself is evident: he refuses to name the apostle John as his authority, and boldly contradicts all other known accounts of Jesus' life. That the Father *also* bears witness to him is something that we must take on faith. John shrewdly places the burden of proof, not on himself as narrator, but on the reader as believer. It is not enough to believe in Jesus; one must believe in the *word* of Jesus, and not in any word, but in *John*'s word.

You do not have his word [or, "the word of him"—*ton logon autou*] abiding in you, for you do not believe him whom he has sent. You search the scriptures [or, "the writings"], because you think that in them you have everlasting life, and it is they that bear witness to me, and yet you do not want to come to me that you may have life. I do not receive glory [or "opinion"—Gr. *doxa*] from men; rather, I know that you have not the love of God within you: I have come in the name of the Father, and you do not receive me; if another comes in his own name, him you will receive. (5:38–43)

Once again, we may hear Jesus and John speaking in unison. John's Logos is the way, the truth, and the life—and he who "climbs in by another way, that man is a thief and a robber" (10:1).

Unlike Matthew, Mark, and Luke, the Gospel of John is conceived "in spirit and in truth." Like the Logos of God, John's word, which seems to come last, has actually existed since the beginning; like the bread of life, it has come down "from above"; like Jesus' inner robe, his Gospel is "woven throughout from above" (Gk. *anō-then*). His Gospel is prior to all. And herein lies John's superiority to those thieves and robbers who came before: their Gospels were of the letter, whereas his is pneumatic, that is, allegorical and spiritual. That John's Gospel is less literal than the synoptics is hardly a fresh observation. It is everywhere said, except by Protestant fundamentalists, that John's Gospel is insistently allegorical and that he shows a casual disregard for historical accuracy. But such statements distort John's design as much as the fundamentalist's refusal to see either the allegory or the contradictions. John is not a blind follower of Philo, or of the epistler of Hebrews. His is allegory with a difference; John's is allegorized narrative which the writer himself takes for the literal historical truth. John trusts that if all were known, he'd be proved right in every detail—he feels it in his bones. Word by word, the Logos has been revealed to him by the indwelling Father and Son. There is no point in trying to go back and check him against some hypothetical or poorly remembered historical "fact." John's word perfectly recovers the "what was" of time. Where Matthew, Mark, and Luke contradict him, they are simply wrong; and if we need proof, we need only look at how clearly the deeds of Jesus' life, as related by John, figure forth doctrinal truths in a way that the synoptic accounts can never hope to match. The implicit allegory is the *guarantee* of his narrative's historical accuracy. This is not to say that the synoptic Gospels are worthless, but only that they have been superseded (and preceded) by the eternally present Logos of John. John's relationship to Mark, for example, is that of Jesus to Moses: "If you do not believe his (literal) *grammasin*, how will you believe my (spiritual) *rēmasin*?" (5:47).[2]

Jesus' sheep hear his voice, and they follow him. John's anxiety is that he will *not* be followed, only preceded, that his pneumatic Gospel will be rejected for the literal, thing-centered Gospels which came before. It is interesting to note that in John, whenever Jesus speaks an allegory, God's chosen people take up stones to stone him, as if to confound his allegory with a supremely literal object. John, too, must fear the stones of the literally minded. Nevertheless, John is not writing fiction. He never thinks of his Gospel as mere parable, as a narrative written to *illustrate* the truth. John, in fact, scorns parable, as does the Jesus of John's Gospel. The synoptics are the storytellers. John has nothing to tell but the truth itself—and he underscores the point with his revision of the Lazarus story: John breathes into Luke's Lazarus the breath of life, transforms him, fashions a dead parchment into a living soul. Next his "real" Lazarus is brought to life by Jesus, as Luke's was not. "Unbind him," says Jesus, "and let him go" (11:44). Nor was John's Lazarus ever "in the bosom" of father Abraham (Lk.16:22ff.), for "No man has gone up to heaven except he who came down from heaven, that is, the Son of man" (Jn. 3:13). Moreover, Luke's father Abraham is wrong in assuming that "If they do not hear Moses and the prophets, neither will they be convinced if someone should rise from the dead" (Lk. 16:31), for John not only resurrects Lazarus, but reports that "on account of him many of the Jews went along and believed in Jesus" (12:10–11)—and the published report of Lazarus' resurrection, says John, caused a second crowd to believe, larger than the first (12:17–18). But the disparity between the two Lazarus stories of Luke and John does not mean that John's is a fiction. Quite the reverse: Jesus really *did* raise Lazarus from the dead, but Luke turned the miracle into a pathetic fiction, a "parable," to illustrate a supposed truth. John thereby turns the narrative tables upon his predecessor. In a similar vein, the Jews' false rhetorical ploy of the woman with seven husbands becomes in John's hands a real woman (about whom more later) who in turn stands as a figure for the Jews themselves.

John everwhere is at pains to tell the *true* history of Jesus' life, as opposed to the stories and rumors circulated by his forebears. For example, in the Petrine gospel of Mark, when Jesus' "soul is anguished, even to death," he prays to the Father, saying, "All things are possible for you. Remove this cup from me" (Mk. 14:34, 36). Though the Son does submit, there is a conflict between his will and that of the Father: "Yet it is *not* what *I*, but what *you*, desire" (14:36). John's Jesus is far more resolute: "Now is my soul troubled. And what shall I say? 'Father, save me from this hour'? No! it is for this very purpose that I have come to this hour!" (Jn. 12:27). John deplores Mark's slander on the Son. Jesus must therefore turn directly to Peter in the Garden and rebuke him, saying, "Shall I not drink the cup which the Father has given me?" (18:11). He shall, and without complaining.

There are other differences. Jesus here does not preach repentance, prophesy of the end times, or debate with Jewish leaders concerning death, divorce, taxes, prayer, sabbath-keeping, burnt offerings, and charitable giving. More importantly, he is not evasive when asked whence his authority derives. The verbal sparring is for Matthew, Mark, and Luke; John's Jesus says plainly that his authority is from the Father. Nor does he refuse to give the Jews a sign. In the synoptics, "signs" (Gk. *sēmeia*) are given only by "false Christs and false prophets" and by Judas, "the betrayer" (e.g., Mt. 24:24; 26:48). Jesus there refuses to give any sign save the *sēmeion* of Jonah. In John, on the other hand, "signs" are Jesus' hallmark. He performs so many that the world itself can not contain them, and on account of his signs there are many who believe, and follow.

John's Jesus is in every way less *Jewish*. He does not exorcise demons (a Jewish custom), nor does he call the Jews his "children," and the Gentiles, "dogs." He, in turn, is never called "Rabbi" except by those who fail fully to understand the truth. And here, despite the assertions of Matthew and Luke to the contrary, the Law of Moses is strictly for the Jews and has no authority over the followers of Christ (Jn. 8:17; 10:34; 15:25; 19:7; cf. Mt. 5:17–20). Only the Pharisees assume that those who do not know the Law are accursed (Jn. 7:49). Here, the only requirement for eternal life is to believe in him who is sent by the Father (Jn. 6:28–29; cf. Lk. 10:25–28). Nor does Jesus have time for Jewish customs like fasting. Three days after his baptism, while Mark's Jesus is still with wild beasts in the wilderness, fasting and being tempted of Satan, John's Jesus is attending a wedding feast in the village of Cana. If he believes in fasting, he never so much as mentions it; and when, on the other hand, he goes to a Jewish festival such as the Passover or the Feast of Tabernacles, he goes not as a participant, as in the synoptics, but as a missionary. Again, in the Gospels of Matthew, Mark, and Luke, Jesus in every city enters the synagogue to teach. In the narrative portion of John's Gospel, Jesus enters a synagogue only once, to deliver his sermon on the eucharist ("Unless you eat the flesh of the Son of man and drink his blood, you have no life in you. . . .); and he delivers this sermon in a synagogue because the eucharist, with its imagery of blood sacrifice, is for John an all-too-Jewish metaphor, the very un-Jewish notion of drinking blood notwithstanding (6:25–59).

In John's account of the last supper, the eucharist is conspicuous by its absence. John wills to abolish the sacrament of the bread and wine, which was based on a prior Jewish feast, and to supplant it with a new, more specifically Christian sacrament, based on the doctrine that the last shall be first. He makes a concerted effort to displace the largely Jewish rites of Petrine Christianity: Jesus, after first instituting John's belated sacrament of foot-washing, specifically commands his followers to "Do as I have done unto you" (13:15). If the larger Christian community never took to washing one another's feet as enthusiastically as they took to the bread and wine, it is probably not John's fault. Moreover, in the synoptics, the last supper is *itself* a Passover meal (Mk. 14:12ff; and parallels) while in John the supper comes "*before* the feast of the Passover, when Jesus knew that his hour had come" (13:1); the Passover is to be eaten instead on the following day (18:28; 19:14). John thus obliterates the temporal distinction between the Passover and the Passion, so that the Jewish rite does not come first. Jesus is then killed even as the paschal lambs are being slaughtered, as a reminder that the sacrificial lamb of the Old Testament does not come before Christ, or even "prefigure" Christ, but is a dim shadow of the eternally present Christ. It is not even a very adequate metaphor: the

only one ever to call Jesus the sacrificial "Lamb of God" is his
Jewish predecessor (1:29, 36). A lamb is a follower. The Son follows
no one, least of all the fathers of the Jews.

Now if, as we have seen, the evangelist feels ambivalent toward
the son of Zebedee as his spiritual forebear, and toward Matthew,
Mark, and Luke as his evangelistic predecessors, it should perhaps
come as no surprise that he feels a certain diffidence even toward
father *Jesus*. For if Jesus can say, "*I* am the truth," what is there left
for his son John to say? The evangelist, in seeking to carve out a
place for himself as the arbiter of all truth, finds that his place was
originally filled by the Son of God, who necessarily left the world
that John might succeed him: when Jesus is about to go to the
Father, he tells his followers, "I go to prepare a place for you"
(14:3)—but John senses that Jesus had *better* go, or there will be no
place for a new son here on earth; if he stays, there will be no need
for John and his Gospel. As Jesus puts it, "He who believes in me
will produce greater works than these *because* (!) I go to the Father"
(14:12). According to John, Jesus joins the Father *in order that* he
may be succeeded, and surpassed, by his true son. "For this is the
will of my Father," says Jesus, "that every one who sees the Son and
believes in him should have eternal life, and I will raise him up at the
last day" (6:40)—raise *whom* up at the last day? Perhaps, every one
who believes on the Son, come Judgment Day. More importantly,
the "Son" himself, John, the latter-day evangelist. And it appears
from the syntax that the latter meaning is foremost in John's mind.

But when the Lord says, "I and the Father are one," he wields a
blade that cuts both ways. His inheritance as the true Son resolves
the problem of authority for his Gospel ("He who rejects me rejects
my Father also"—15:23), but raises the question of whether his
word is not merely an unnecessary repetition. Jesus as Son finds his
authority in the Father, but must also confess "that the Father is
greater than I" (14:28), for "the Son can do nothing of his own
accord, but only what he sees the Father doing; for whatever he
does, that the Son does in like manner" (5:19). Jesus knows that the
son can at best hope to duplicate the glory of the renowned father,
an insight which sometimes makes for a strangely difficult transition: "Truly, truly, I say to you," says Jesus, "he who receives
whomever I send, receives *me*; and he who receives *me*, receives the

one who sent me. Having said these things, Jesus was troubled in spirit . . ." (13:20–21).

John has no conscious desire to be *greater* than Jesus, but neither does he wish to be a lesser son, or merely a belated repetition. He wants rather to make a significant and original contribution. John therefore shapes a role for himself as the son whose gospel *completes* and *consummates* the life and work of the Son. His unique mission is subtly hinted at in his account of the crucifixion: Jesus was crucified not at the third hour, as in Mark, but at the sixth hour (Mk. 15:25; Jn. 19:14). "After this, Jesus perceiving that all things were now complete, cried, 'I thirst!' " (19:28). This seemingly insignificant addition to the synoptic Gospels recalls the earlier scene in John when at the sixth hour Jesus required water (standing for the Baptist) before he could give the woman (Israel) the gift of the spirit. On that occasion Jesus said, "Whoever drinks of the water that I shall give him will never thirst" (4:14). But John suggests that it is now time for some fresh living water, for Jesus is thirsty. All he gets, however, is sour wine—which in Matthew, Mark, and Luke was merely sour wine but which here comes to stand for the synoptic Gospels themselves. The implication is that the new son must step forward with living water and new wine, for the Scripture, or *graphē*, will not be "made complete" until the true Logos (John's Gospel) is generated from above by the son and heir of the Son of God—so that John may truly say, "My food is to do the will of the one who sent me, and to *complete* his work" (4:34). The point is subtly underscored by earlier passages. At Cana, for example, there were only six pots of water, which, according to biblical numerology, is a sign of imperfection. John's Gospel, a pot of new wine, is the seventh. Similarly, the woman at the well had five lovers. Jesus appeared as the sixth, the spiritual bridegroom, but it is John, the seventh, who completes the tale. Again, the cripple at the Pool of Bethzatha waited as thirty-eight angels came and went. Jesus appeared as the thirty-ninth, but John, the fortieth, is the one who finally points the way to the promised land. It is therefore not until Jesus has named his spiritual heir that he can say, "It is finished" (19:30). "Then, bowing his head, he delivered up his spirit"—not to God in heaven, but to John.

All this might prompt us to ask of John what the Jews asked of

Jesus: Are you greater than our father who died? (8:53). The answer is a qualified "No." In some ways, John does preempt the Son, as for example, in his account of Lazarus. Luke's Lazarus was not resurrected. John's is resurrected twice, as it were, and John's own miracle comes first: "For as the father raises the dead and gives them life, so also the son gives life to whom he will" (5:21). John wills to breathe life into Luke's Lazarus, so that Jesus may follow him in giving life to him as well. But John's "sign" is strictly a symbolic triumph; he knows that he has no power literally to raise men from the dead, or to preempt Jesus.

If John has any Oedipal designs on his spiritual father, he suppresses them. We may return again to the crucifixion scene: "Standing by the cross of Jesus were his mother and his mother's sister, Mary the wife of Clopas and Mary Magdalene," together with that disciple whom Jesus loved (19:25). The carefully balanced parallelism, with one "and" missing, raises the perennial question: are there two women, or four? Is Jesus' mother the wife of "Clopas" ("renowned father"), and is Magdalene her sister? If not, who is this wife of a renowned father, mentioned nowhere but here, in the Fourth Gospel, and why is Jesus' beloved son standing beside her? Jesus may be disturbed by the same thought: for "when Jesus saw [his] mother and [the] disciple whom he loved standing near, he said to the mother, 'Woman, behold, your son!' Then said he to the disciple, 'Behold, your mother!'" (19:26–27)—as if to say, "Woman, remember, this man is not your husband," and "Son, you are not to be a 'renowned father,' but must remain a son."

John seems compelled to remind himself, time and again, that he is not, in fact, greater than his father, the Son: "You must *remember* the word which I spoke to you," says Jesus, "a servant is *not greater* than his lord" (15:20). But if "he who is sent is *not greater* than the one who sends him" (13:16), neither need he be any *less*. John resolves his ambiguous status as son by establishing finally a mystical union between himself and the Logos of God, so that he may partake of the Father's greatness without seeking to preempt the Son in any way:

> He who has seen me has seen the father. How do you say, 'Show us the father'? Do you not believe that I am in the father and the father in me? (14:9–10)

Just as the Word and the Father are one, so is the Word one with John, and John one with the Father. The evangelist dares not seek priority to Jesus. What he seeks rather is a perfect union, a oneness with both Father and Son, that he may be with them "since the beginning." That John and Jesus talk alike, we have already seen; there is no distinction made between the language of one and that of the other. The implied identification, which is hardly accidental, is underscored by John's frequent use of Greeks puns on such words as *logos, sēmeion, ergon, anōthen,* and *akoloutheō.* Jesus' *sēmeia* ("signs") and John's *sēmeia* ("written proofs, letters") are inseparably one. Jesus' word (*ho logos autou*) and John's word *of* him (*ho logos autou*) are identical (4:41; 5:24, 38; 8:31, et al.). Jesus had "done one deed" (*hen ergon epoiēsa*), John has "written one work" (*hen ergon epoiēsa*), and the world marvels (7:21; cf. 9:34; 5:20, 36; 10:25–38; 14:10–12).

Jesus' metaphors likewise refer equally to himself and to that son with whom he is at one: "A woman giving birth is distressed," he says, "for her hour has come; but when she brings forth the child she no longer remembers her anguish, for joy that a child is born into the world" (16:21). But then the metaphor seems to get confused: "Now, then, *you* are distressed—but I will see you again, and your hearts will have joy, and no one will take your joy from you" (16:22). It's as if Jesus, whose hour has come (12:23; 13:1), must labor to produce a child to take his place in the world, that his joy may be full. The child in turn (specifically, John) must then give birth, not to a new child, but to a returning Jesus, that *his* joy may be full. The true Son, having vanished from the world, is to be brought back into the world through his child, John. Again, if "he who enters by the door is the shepherd of the sheep" (10:2), who is the door? Jesus says, "I am the door of the sheep" (10:8). Who, then, is the shepherd? Jesus and John are one door, one shepherd. Jesus is the door who admits John into the kingdom; John in turn is the door who brings the true Jesus back into the world, as in the metaphor of the woman in travail. Jesus is the shepherd who becomes the Lamb; John is a following lamb who becomes the shepherd, he in the father and the father in him. John serves the Son by following him; and the Son in turn serves John, serves him as a trope for *John himself*— perhaps the most audacious substitution in the history of our literature. John thus takes his place as the third member of an everlasting trinity: Father, Son, and the son of the Son. John is that logos from above which was in the beginning with God, and, in a sense, was God, from the first moment of creation.

The logos which creates all things is not, after all, that of the Father, but rather is that of the Son, at once the logos of Christ and the logos of John:

> This very logos was in the beginning with God: all things came into being through the logos, and without it there came not one thing into the world. That which has come into being was life in the logos, and the life was the light of men. (1:2–4)

Through John's eternally present, infinitely creative word, a whole world has come into being. He, along with God and the *P* writer of Genesis, creates through the power of the word itself: "Let there be light"—and there was light. His transcendent word is prior to all other beginnings, narrative or otherwise, prior to the synoptics, to the son of Zebedee, to John the Baptist, to the prophets, Moses, and Abraham. And there is a sense in which even the Father himself must follow the all-fathering word of John, for it is John's word which declares him. Without the logos, nothing of God may be known. John the evangelist, though belated, is the prime mover whose word establishes the world. Our only task, and the only requirement for us to enter the kingdom of John's heaven, is that we learn to follow.

NOTES

1. Never does the phrase *gennēthēnai anōthen* mean "born again" as in the fundamentalist slogan. In fact, "again" is precisely what "*anōthen* does *not* mean; it is a term which denotes, not repetition, but a higher place or earlier time. Reducing the phrase *gennēthēnai anōthen* to the "born again" formula obscures the meaning, which strongly suggests that one must overcome *what has been*, which is what Jesus' Gospel (and John's) offers.
2. As it turns out, of course, John *was* followed—by the redactor of chapter 21. It is clear now that the writer of chapters 1–20 has died, but there is another Johannine writer to carry on, one who seeks to demonstrate that revelation did not end with John the evangelist, but will continue: "After this Jesus revealed himself *again* to the disciples . . . this was now the *third* time that Jesus was revealed" (21:1, 14). The redactor imitates father John:

while the beloved disciple waits behind, Peter dives in and arrives first, only to learn that Jesus seems to doubt both his love and his resolve as a shepherd; moreover, another will gird him and carry him where he does not wish to go; Peter will perish, John will survive him, and it is none of his business. "And there are many other things which Jesus did," writes the redactor in the conclusion to his postscript, "which, if they were to be written one by one, I suppose that the world itself could not contain all the scrolls written." In Johannine Christianity, Jesus' earthly ministry does not proscribe the religion's assimilation of future (that is, belated) revelations (cf. John's Jesus: "I have many things to tell you, but you cannot bear them now" 26:12). According to the redactor, there is room even for the son of the son of the Son.

Biblical Narrative
and Modern Consciousness

HERBERT N. SCHNEIDAU

The first point I want to make is one that is implicit in much else in this volume: that narrative is of the essence, if one may use the term, of the Bible, it is not merely a vehicle or adjunct or epipheomenon. This point needs emphasis because it tends to be eclipsed by the assumption that the Bible consists of a set of doctrinal propositions, with illustrative stories: of all the *idées reçues* about the Bible, this one is surely the most stultifying. Probably most of those who read the Bible, speaking statistically, do so to find doctrinal guidance, or to buttress already fixed precepts. Yet this exercise effaces the storial character, and hinders recognition of some important consequences of that. The framers of the Pentateuchal laws were wiser, who put them all into a narrative framework, and thus showed that they recognized what they had in hand.

Even theologians whose interest is primarily in doctrinal questions can recognize the danger of treating the narratives as merely instrumental. James Barr poses for himself the question of why the Bible was for believers so "unquestionedly central, so inevitable and necessary, so sufficient and so authoritative?" And the answer, he says, "lies in the literary character of the Bible . . . [for it] is not in itself a work of doctrine or theology."

In a sense—surprising as it seems to say it—the Bible, or most of it, is not concerned to enunciate ultimate truth. Its concern is more with something contingent. . . . Interlaced as the whole is with theology, theology or doctrine is not the prime form in which it speaks. It speaks rather in the voice of a people's hymns in praise of its God, in the moral instructions or counsels of its teachers, in the utterances of the prophets for such and such a time, in letters and occasional papers, but most of all, of course, in narrative. Narrative story is, as has been so widely recognized, the most typical of all the Bible's literary forms . . . the Bible speaks to and for a much wider range of human experience and questioning than does any doctrinal formulation, however otherwise accurate.[1]

But Barr does not comprehend the full significance of his own observations; he fails to make clear that the narratives transcend, even evade, theology, more surely than they serve as vivid embodiment or dramatization of it. As Harold Bloom observes, there is really no Jewish theology before Philo. If J is a writer more inescapable than Shakespeare and more pervasive in our consciousness than Freud, it is because his uncanny Yahweh escapes formulation.

To pursue this escape, let us begin by putting the question of narrative as broadly as possible. What about the frequently heard assertion, nowadays, that narrative as such has to do with the very core of human experience? Does narrative typify the Bible not so much because it records the beliefs of a people in a compelling form, but because it recapitulates the linguistic nature and structure of our being? Is not man the linguistic animal? "Who says man says culture and who says culture says language," says Claude Lévi-Strauss, and Walker Percy puts the case almost as pithily:

Why is it that every normal man on earth speaks, that is, can utter an unlimited number of sentences in a complex language, and that not one single beast has ever uttered a word?

Why are there not some "higher" animals which have acquired a primitive language?

Why are there not some "lower" men who speak a crude, primitive language?

Why is there no such thing as a primitive language?

Why is there such a gap between nonspeaking animals and speaking man, when there is no other such gap in nature?

How can a child learn to speak a language in three years without anyone taking trouble about it . . . while a great deal of time and trouble is required to teach a chimpanzee a few hand signals?[2]

Percy's lifework is based on his conviction that man's whole problem is to come to terms with the fact that he is the unique linguistic animal. Given how difficult it would be to keep a child from learning language, it is not enough to define man as the language-using animal: it would be more true to the facts to say that language is man-using. For it is not a tool that we can pick up and lay down at will. It's more like a pandemic; we cannot opt out of life in a verbal universe. "We come to our studies from a culture where the instrumental view of language is dominant," says D. S. Carne-Ross, but he prefers Heidegger's reversal: "Language uses us."[3] Heidegger's aphorism has a homely parallel in the saying that a hen is only an egg's way of making another egg: DNA reproduces creatures for the sake of more DNA, which is a form of language.

If we grant the linguistic nature of man, we may find a certain plausibility in suggestions by Julian Jaynes about what he calls "narratizing" and its function in, or as, consciousness. He points out that at some subconscious level we are always weaving a story, always at least latently verbal, out of all that we encounter and how we interpret it. "In consciousness, we are always seeing our vicarial selves as the main figures in the stories of our lives," he says, meaning by "vicarial self" the projection or analogical image of ourselves that is the product of self-consciousness.[4] "But it is not just our own analog 'I' that we are narratizing; it is everything else in consciousness. A stray fact is narratized to fit with some other stray fact," even if we don't really notice them. Just as the brain inverts, organizes, and schematizes a pattern of smears on our retinas to produce a visual field, so the submerged narratizing that Jaynes postulates may knit together scattered perceptions, synthesizing them with hypothetical scenarios into an awareness of our surroundings.

Jaynes points out that our remembered sensations of such simple acts as entering a room, or swimming in a pool, consist of "created imagery''—not genuine recall of what it actually felt like, but projection of a kinesthetic image of what we imagine when we reconstruct the event. "Memory is the medium of the must-have-been," he observes. It is much easier to see ourselves doing things than to really remember them, if indeed that can be done at all. But if memory is a matter of created imagery, what about actual experience? Is there narratizing there too? Yes, and it may be that "primary sensation" is an illusion of our self-told stories. Jacques Derrida has shown that all human experience is "inseparable from this field of the mark, which is to say, from the network of effacement and of difference, of units of iterability, which are separable from their internal and external context and also from themselves, inasmuch as the very iterability which constituted their identity does not permit them ever to be a unity that is identical to itself. . . . There is no experience consisting of *pure* presence but only of chains of differential marks."[5] In other words, any experience that does not comprise merely unrecognizable or unassimilable sensation must have mediated, language-like qualities; it cannot mean anything all by itself but must take its place in the field of diacritical, marked differences that constitute the possibility of language. To be assimilable, any experience must be potentially iterable, and thus not uniquely and solely itself, and not its own meaning. Any sensation without these linguistic characteristics would be meaningless: to bring in the concept of meaning is to make experience a kind of proto-language, in fact a proto-writing. "From the moment that there is meaning there are nothing but signs."[6] Compare the Bradleyan paradoxes that fascinated T. S. Eliot: "No actual experience could be merely immediate, for if it were, we should certainly know nothing about it. . . . In order that it should be feeling at all, it must be conscious, but so far as it is conscious it ceases to be merely feeling."[7]

If a linguistic substratum underlies experience, and if consciousness should be seen as a processing in latently verbal terms, then Jaynes's idea of narratizing means that we should rethink our concepts of perception. Perhaps not many of us go as far as James Joyce's Mr. Duffy, who has a habit of composing "in his mind from time to time a short sentence about himself containing a subject in the third person and a predicate in the past tense," but I think we can all recognize the syndrome. Very likely the synthetic and creative element in perception, so familiar to students of literature from Coleridge's theory of imagination, involves in man at least a kind of subliminal story: each look at things employs what E. H. Gombrich calls *schemata* to deal with what we expect to perceive, how it goes together, and what it means. Indeed the whole process is one of interpretation, and narrative is probably the most fundamental form of interpretation, as in midrashic fillings-out of Biblical lacunae. If experience as well as recall takes place in an essentially narrative mode, that would go far to explain why human beings react so sensitively and imaginatively to all sorts of narratives. Even children's tales can catch us up, give us a sense of participation and immediacy: to keep readers from projecting themselves into narratives, a writer has to employ deliberate deadening techniques, as in police or military reports. Otherwise stories take on a life of their own that can become all too real, for people of all ages. Whoever has watched a group listening to a story knows how human beings can participate in it even to the point of collective delusion. What else should we call it when a storyteller makes us jump with sudden fear, or recoil in horror or disgust, or yearn with desire, on cue? Even a narrative that otherwise repels us, for some moral or aesthetic reason, can keep our attention, so overmastering is our desire to know "how it comes out"—that is, how some resolution can finally release us from our self-projections: our "sense of an ending" does not come from a barren formalist impulse but from a need to recover emotional freedom. A narrative is a managed and cued fantasy into which we project so readily that we can all recognize ourselves in Tolstoy's countess who wept for the heroine throughout the opera, while her coachman waiting outside froze to death.

This story also speaks to the point that stories have a way of tapping those feelings that we habitually anesthetize. Partly, no doubt, this happens because we know that indulging these feelings will cost us nothing: it's only a story. Yet we have some persuasive inducements to question whether this is really the whole story: if we work further on it, we might begin to wonder if represented experience is not in fact more powerful than actual experience. José Ortega y Gasset made a variant of the point when he noted that what moves us in a novel is not the "reality" depicted but the representation of it: in real life Madame Bovary's company would be excruciatingly boring, but in the novel it's a different story. Marcel Proust's great work takes the power of representation as theme: like the magic lantern of his childhood, he shows us a procession of figures, each illustrating ways of being governed by mediated experience. René Girard analyzed the *snobbisme* that so often appears as one of these ways, but we should add the motifs in which stories of one kind or another control desires and destinies: as when Swann, struggling to master his jealousy of Odette, is undone by a few ambiguous words in a letter.[8]

If we think of consciousness as a submerged narrative-processing of experience, this can also help explain other features of it, such as the fact that it distracts from or interferes with many of our acts. If we try to play the piano, or utter speech, or remember a name or the words to a song, consciousness may inhibit or even cripple our performance: it distracts just as a story told to us would. Jaynes even argues that consciousness interferes with thinking! Without rehearsing the argument, I will simply assert that many such points suggest just how intertwined are represented and direct experience for us. The phenomena of hypnotism, on which Jaynes has a provocative chapter, seem to show that when our inner narratives are manipulated we can do things we "never thought of doing":

> If I ask you to taste vinegar as champagne, to feel pleasure when I jab a pin in your arm, or to stare into darkness and contract the pupils of your eyes to an imagined light, or to wilfully and really believe something you do not ordinarily believe, just anything, you would find these tasks difficult if not impossible. But if I first put you through the induction procedures of hypnosis, you could accomplish all these things at my asking without any effort whatever.

Not only hypnotism but its history is demonstrative:

> [Mesmer's] cures were effective because he had explained his exotic theory to his patients with vigorous conviction. The violent seizures and peculiar twists of sensations at the application of magnets were all due to a cognitive imperative that these things would happen, which they did, constituting a kind of self-perpetu-

ating escalating 'proof' that the magnets were working and could effect a cure. . . . As beliefs about hypnosis changed, so also its very nature. A few decades after Mesmer, subjects no longer twisted with strange sensations and convulsions. Instead they began spontaneously to speak and reply to questions during their trance state. Nothing like this had happened before. . . . In the middle of the [nineteenth] century, phrenology, the mistaken idea that conformations of the skull indicate mental faculties, became so popular that it actually engulfed hypnosis for a time. Pressure on the scalp over a phrenological area during hypnosis caused the subject to express the faculty controlled by that area (yes, this actually happened), a phenomenon never seen before or since.

Apparently it is still easy to show how expectation controls what happens in hypnosis. Subjects' behavior in trances can be correlated with what they believe, or are told in an authoritative way: "For example, an introductory psychology class was casually told that under hypnosis a subject's dominant hand cannot be moved. This had never occurred in hypnosis in any era. It was a lie. Nevertheless, when members of the class at a later time were hypnotized, the majority, without any coaching or further suggestion, were unable to move their dominant hand."[9] Among other points, Jaynes notes that hypnotic expectation and behavior is enhanced by crowds, as in theaters; by childhood religious training, and authoritative punishment; and by the invention of imaginary companions in childhood. Surely narrative and fantasy are implicated here, as they would be in such well-attested phenomena as faith healing and the placebo effect.

Hugh Kenner holds that Joyce's earliest and most constant insight, the enabling act of his work, was that "people live in stories that structure their world.[10] Perhaps it is easier to see this in Ireland than most places. Here Kenner is discussing "Eveline," who like Don Quixote or Madame Bovary is a victim of fantasies engendered by the diffusion and confusion of certain sentimental scenarios, in her case "shopgirls' romances in magazines." But the principle is ubiquitous in Joyce's work; and another Irishman, John Dominic Crossan, has given us the wonderful formulation that we live in language, and in story, as fish live in the sea.[11] Some, however, go even further.

> [Jacques] Lacan has offered a way of conceiving of the human being or subject as developing as an effect of the symbolic processes in which it may be articulated, and is therefore no longer situated . . . outside its observed structures and discourses in a position of fixed and controlling specularity (maintaining the distinction *percipiens* and *perceptum*), but is rather the effect of a specific production, a history of acts of coming into place from which observations or discourses are possible. The subject is now continually implicated in the field of its own enunciations.[12]

Lacan, and his interpreters, resist translation back into a more demotic idiom, partly for good reasons. But here is a targum: "We consist of the stories we tell of, and to, ourselves." Story is not only the sea but the fish.

Here we are looking at the universality of narrative in human affairs, but what about the particularity of the biblical narratives in our culture? Is there anything special about these stories, not only about their content but about the way they are told, that sets them apart and makes them characteristic of Western culture? Perhaps the most thought-provoking aspect of Jaynes's work, indeed, is his suggestion that what we call "consciousness" is a learned linguistic behavior rather than an inherent substrate of human mental activity. He hypothesizes that men before the first millennium B.C. did not "think out" their reactions to situations, but rather reacted to superegoistic voices from the right hemisphere of their brains. These voices told them what to do, just like the voices of modern schizophrenics, and Jaynes concludes that schizophrenia was in effect the normal condition in the age of theophanies (the voices would of course be attributed to gods). Faced with a typical modern problem like a traffic jam, "our bicameral [or ancient schizoid] man would not do what you and I would do, that is, quickly and efficiently swivel our consciousness over to the matter and narratize out what to do. He would have to wait for his bicameral voice which with the stored-up admonitory wisdom of his life would tell him nonconsciously what to do."[13] For our purposes we can leave this bicameral thesis aside as merely arguable—it's the weakest part of the book, although it is the organizing thesis—and dispensable, but the suggestion that our kind of consciousness is not innate or intrinsic deserves further consideration. By this train of thought, a narrative mode of perceptual processing would be predictable in man, given the fact of language, but the identity of Western man would have something to do with a special adaptation, or perhaps hypertrophy of that mode into a behavior that lets us narratize out what to do.

We know that in all cultures, our own not excepted, there is a constant self-deceptive urge to rationalize (or rather to accept without scrutiny) all procedures and institutions as natural, given, part of the order of things, to be taken for granted. Cultures that did not have such urges could not last long; they would dissolve in the acids of self-doubt and self-questioning. Satisfying these impulses toward "naturalization," according to Roland Barthes and others, must be one of the major functions of myth and oral tradition: if these act as kinds of DNA for cultures, enabling their continual self-replication, they do so by putting the culture's forms into codes that can be learned, and cybernetically used as a self-governing system. With the myths' narrative as vehicle, the culture can teach each generation how things are done, and oral tradition can provide feedback that locks in the precepts. Suppose, however, that our kind of consciousness is a peculiar Western adaptation of narrative for situations that ancient forms of thinking, whatever they were, dealt with differently. Might it not be that the powerful kind of self-criticism which is our individual and collective legacy from the Hebrew prophets have something to do with an individualistic internalizing of narrative, self-questioning and self-answering, and that this has become our dominant mode of thought? The self-probing of our motives and the calling into question of the sacred cows of our culture that the prophets urge on us may have taken hold in a need to weave private stories, more and more comprehensively, out of our experiences, making the outer into the inner. Carne-Ross complains that such kinds of subjectivizing have impoverished our cultural tradition, repealing the various Copernican revolutions that seem to rebuke our anthropocentric view of things but in which paradoxically we take so much pride: he calls this the "great principle of inwardness or internalization that has put man at the center of things and laid waste the visible world."[14] (Of this paradox Reinhold Niebuhr remarked that "the vantage point from which man judges his insignificance is a rather significant vantage point"; even in our self-rebuke there is a self-enthronement.)[15] Whether we thus pervert the prophets' message is not my question here; I want only to remark on their relevance for any analysis of the aetiology of "the great principle of . . . internalization." For although we know that all cultures use stories, sayings, myths, and legends as armatures on which to structure teachings, the accounts we receive of these activities from students of other cultures generally stress the predominance of collective participation in them: there seems to be little private self-storytelling involved. But our heritage comprises both the prophets and those Greek philosophers who, on Eric Havelock's showing, urged a dissolution of the oralist tradition of the poets, that is, the myths and epics that served to indoctrinate Greek schoolboys.[16] Plato apparently led the fight for liberation from the old ways and old solidarities, prescribing instead an individualistic, critical examination of pieties and truisms. When this intellectual force joined that of the prophets, our pattern of thought became "modern," real inwardness was born. Bruno Snell relates the birth of the inner self or soul to self-objectification as we find it in, say, the poems of Sappho.[17] But it took Plato and the Bible to make general the kind of "soul," always anxiously examining its own moral status, that has prevailed in our tradition and that fits so well a concept of internalized narratizing.

We can expand this line of inquiry in a way that marks the Bible's narratives as specifically determinative for our heritage. However, an excursus is in order here on the whole vexed problem of finding valid differences between Western and other traditions, and then deciding if these are related to the distinctiveness, if any, of ancient Israel. Both parts of the project are being sharply questioned today, as residue from a discredited ethnocentrism. H. W. F. Saggs says:

> "There are basically two types of religion—our own, and the religions of other peoples." This is an implicit premise not unknown in the study of ancient Near Eastern religions. Not infrequently a "we"–"they" dichotomy manifests itself in such studies, with Israelite religion, accepted as an element in the western cultural tradition, regarded as standing with us on one side of a dividing line; beyond that line stand those religions which are both

strange and false. . . . All this is legitimate, provided the theological value judgements are recognized as such, and not passed off as
religio-historical judgements. However, cases are not infrequent in
which even the most distinguished scholars are guilty of blurring
this distinction.[18]

Who could deny the last assertion? Yet all Saggs's examples are
taken from an earlier generation; today, so anxious are we all to
disclaim ethnocentrism, the situation is nearly opposite. Prevailing
attitudes make it difficult to discuss the issues on their merits.
Although I lament the passing of ethnocentrism no more than
anyone else, I still think there are significant differences between
our tradition and others that must be explained, though they are not
superiorities except in highly contingent senses; and frankly I find
the most compelling parts of Saggs's arguments to be his conces-
sions to the other point of view. Some of his passages make a good
case for Israelite or rather biblical-prophetic distinctiveness. But he
argues predominantly the other way.

Part of the problem is the vogue of structuralism, in the Lévi-
Straussian sense. We should remember that such structuralism is
programmed to find many patterns of similarity between cultures,
and thus its devaluing and debunking of Western differences is
predictable, even smacks of self-fulfilling prophecy. The blurring
out of differences is a consequence of methods employed: superbly
adapted to deal with oral traditions, in which the lathe of communal
transmission removes aberrant individualisms, they have neither
recognition of nor use for the kind of particularities that concern us
here. Structuralism's polemic against ethnocentrism has been of
great value, but if we erect it into an orthodoxy, we will forget its
tendentious character.

Obviously there is a sense in which we are all self-deluded and
programmed or determined to produce defenses of obsolete views,
just as there is a sense in which all human cultures are simply
variations on one model. Within any culture there must be powerful
rationalizing and naturalizing forces, ceaselessly validating the accepted ways of doing things: as remarked earlier, a society without
such forces would be self-corrosive. Yet it is precisely the presence
of an opposing, self-critical impetus within our tradition that raises

most urgently the question of difference. Surely this impetus was what produced anthropology and ultimately structuralism, as Lévi-Strauss leads us (but not himself) to see in the last chapters of *Tristes Tropiques*. Whereas if structuralism's premises are all true, and human thought is simply cybernetic variation on patterns needed to keep the culture ongoing and self-identical and self-reinforcing, then how account for such penetrating self-analysis as structuralism?

That the biblical narratives are indeed distinctive is of course the thesis of Erich Auerbach's famous essay in *Mimesis*, comparing Homer's style to that of Genesis. Classicists have attacked it, bridling at such assertions as the one that Homer "knows no background."[19] But Auerbach's categorization of Homer characters—vital but fixed, unchanging even in their power—seems sufficiently accurate to make the relevant point: there is something developmental and "historical" about the biblical figures even when they are clearly drawn from the world of legend. In part this effect is due to the notorious inconsistencies of the text, those seams and joins that expose the tacking-together of disparate traditions, providing such contorted problems of interpretation: these have the provocative effect of suggesting problematic "background" and evolution for the characters, and of giving them thereby a depth of individuality unknown to the Homeric heroes. Whereas "Odysseus on his return is virtually the same as when he left twenty years earlier," Jacob and David truly age, wax and wane, and become unforgettably vivid in the process. Manifestly we derive our canons of "realism" from this aspect of biblical narrative; but also here we see that the patriarchs, the claimants to the kingship, even many of the minor figures have a latent innerness, ascribable to the same processes that produce their "background," that marks them off from the Homeric heroes and from the denizens of myth. We never wonder what Odysseus is thinking; if he conceals crafty mental reservations (his vaunted wisdom consists mainly in never giving his right name to strangers, and in always lying unless he sees more compelling reason to tell the truth—qualities that cause Athena to compare him to the gods), Homer always tells us what they are; they are not private to him. But in the Bible inwardness is powerfully suggested by a kind of *pointilliste* technique, forcing the reader's imagination into interpretive acts. This is one more link to add to those by which Frank Kermode in *The Genesis of Secrecy* brings together the Bible's narratives and modernist ("fractured," elliptical, Impressionist) literature.

These tales of the Bible were originally written so as to be read to a group, in all likelihood; their world was assuredly oralist, and private reading would have been anomalous. Yet compared with the songs of Homer the oral-formulaic bard mesmerizing his audience with Achean glories, they contain latently private readings, and at least since Luther made "every man his own priest" they have nurtured the spiritual fantasies of generations of inwardlooking, private individuals. They have the quality of appearing to be what Homer's narratives can be only with great strain: messages fraught with intensely personal guidance. The acts of Achilles may have served to show Greek schoolboys that they should all pant after self-glorifications (see Havelock plus Philip Slater, *The Glory of Hera*) but they cannot be seen as containing urgent counsels from God to our particular, individual souls. For the Greeks, as for medieval and Renaissance mythography, Achilles was a universal example: the type of the warrior consumed by desire for *arete*. But except in the interpretations of Philo and his followers, the Bible does not give us types in that essentialist sense.

Robert Alter makes a similar point, extending Auerbach's insights, in his recent *Art of Biblical Narrative*. Pointing out that the characters of the Bible cannot have "fixed Homeric epithets," because of their capacity for change and development and unpredictable, even paradoxical acts, Alter contrasts the scene of Priam begging Achilles for Hector's body with that of David mourning his son by Bathsheba. In the *Iliad*, Priam kisses the hand that has killed his son, and weeps; and Achilles weeps too, remembering his own father and his lover Patroclus. "In the view of the Greek poet, there are universal emotions, universal facts of existence, shared by all men, and Priam's plea has reminded Achilles that, though they are separated by enmity and age, they share identically in this human heritage of relation and feeling." With this essentialist behavior compare the scene in 2 Samuel 12:19–24. David prostrates himself while the child lies sick, tearing his garments and refusing to eat, but when the fearful servants admit to him that the child has died, David arises, washes, and eats. Which astounds the servants, and of course the readers, while the style of narrative revelation with its enigmatic ellipses and laconic, "starkly eloquent words of explanation" reinforces our wonder. David, "so bleakly aware of his own inevitable mortality as he mourns for his dead son," says as he rouses himself "I shall go to him, but he will not return to me." Alter concludes: "All men may indeed grieve over the loss of their loved ones, but this universal fact does not produce a universal response because the expression of feeling, the very experience of feeling, takes place through the whorled and deeply grained medium of each person's stubborn individuality."[20] We recognize here the lifelike in the paradoxical, the universal in the particular. E. H. Gombrich, in contesting Sir Joshua Reynolds' essentialist notion of "generality" as artistic value, points to the wax figure of the guard at Madame Tussaud's: "The figure on the staircase made to hoax the visitor simply represents 'an' attendant, one member of a class. It stands there as a 'substitute' for the expected guard—but it is not more 'generalized' in Reynolds' sense [than the "portraits of the great" in the galleries].[21] No less than the famous figures, or David, the guard must be particular before he can be universal. Joyce used exactly this phrase—"in the particular is contained the universal"—in explaining why he always wrote about Dublin: another link of the Bible to modernism.[22]

What Homeric narratives have that the Bible lacks, in the largest sense, is the underlying concept of a *logos*, a cosmic constitution or blueprint, ultimately a rational and verbal principle in that it can be apprehended by the perfected soul through the enunciation of eternal verities. The universalism and essentialism of Homeric style, which is also reflected in the typifying or originary situations in myth in general, premises a logocentric cosmos in which even the gods themselves function with great regularity, as Bruno Snell noted, and all beings behave according to their inherent "natures." This world has no real concept of development, but consists of endless repetitions of cycles. Cities rise and fall, gods punish and reward, animals and men live out their patterned lives, although men may achieve greater or lesser happiness by the degree to which they are entuned to this cosmic wisdom. The *logos* in this sense (not in John's, obviously) is the most sophisticated of all the attempts at "naturalization," seeking to found society on the rock of the given, the *de rerum natura*. It corresponds as Bloom points out to some late concepts of the *Torah* and to Freud's notion of the psyche: everything is in it. Hence Freud is a religious writer while J is not, at least in the logocentric sense.

Lévi-Strauss concludes that the hidden refrain of the Oedipus myth (and, he seems to imply, of all myth) is this: "Social life validates cosmology by its similarity of structure. Hence cosmology is true."[23] The circular reasoning implicit in myth guarantees the validity on the culture by aligning the cosmos and the social order as harmonic and mutually reinforcing; typically it finds the origins of things cultural in nature, and sometimes vice versa. Contrast the biblical view of things, in which as Henri Frankfort observes there is positive delight in contemplating reversals or upsets of the social order—which receives no validation from cosmology, and is emphatically not a manifestation of the nature of things: in fact the last shall be first, and so on.[24] Neither in the world of myth nor anywhere in the great early civilizations, and certainly not in Homer, is there a concept of change as anything other than superficial or even delusive. Frankfort says of Egypt that there "only the changeless was truly significant," and Saggs says of Mesopotamia:

> Conservatism does not necessarily imply stasis, and new developments both in religious concepts and in technology could and did arise in Mesopotamia in the first millennium. But Mesopotamian conservatism had the consequence that the new did not lead to rejection of the old; rather, the old continued to exist alongside the new. . . . Changes in Mesopotamian religion did come about, but they were neither presented nor seen as changes.[25]

Compare the attacks of Amos, Isaiah, Jeremiah, and Ezekiel on old sayings and proverbs in Israel: "For though your people Israel be as the sand of the sea, only a remnant of them will return" [Isa. 10:22; cf. Gen. 22:17].[26]

The discounting of change as merely apparent meant of course that any concept of history that emerged was limited to minor significance: Aristotle counted poetry more philosophic than history because the latter was limited to what actually happened, whereas poetry can manifest the *logos* in all that *might* have happened. The interest of the Oedipus story is in some deep pattern underlying the events, and even of such concepts—*hubris, nemesis*, and the rest—that we may use to deal with them; the revelation of the pattern may be breathtaking, but it cannot bring us news in any historical sense, since nothing is ever really new; our reaction must be a shock of recognition: ah yes, that's what was inevitable from the start if only we could have seen it. Only the thickness of our earthbound sight, as in Plato's cave, prevents our apprehension of the *logos* in all things: if men could really see the good, the true, and the beautiful they would inevitably desire it, and harmony could reign throughout the chain of being: history would never even happen. In Stoicism, the logical end product of this thought, one isolates oneself from the deceptive vicissitudes of history and fortune (a view that in Western history dominates only in the Middle Ages, which also believed that the cosmology reinforced the social order and therefore represents a mythological hiatus in our tradition, mediated by the Hellenizing Fathers).[27]

Manifestly this vision conflicts with the biblical one, where no view of cyclical repetition appears except in the foreign-influenced Wisdom books. Things do not run according to their natures but as Yahweh chooses. Thus history is vital, because it is the record of his choices as his unpredictable, bewildering "mighty hand" cuts across the expectations and preconceptions and best-laid plans of men. History in the Bible accords with such themes as the rise of the Younger Son, on whom inexplicable favor descends in spite of primogeniture, appearance, strength, and so forth; the Reluctant Leader, a shy retiring figure suddenly thrust by Yahweh into prominence; the fall of the mighty, the last becoming first, and so on. For his plans Yahweh chooses frail vessels, not those of obvious merits, and his dealings with them are full of uncanniness. History has no *logos* to manifest; with a God so inexplicable, so remote, and yet so interventionist, there can be no cosmic constitution to which man may conform if he sees clearly (again the sapiential books are cross-grained). The blindness of human vision is not the problem. What separates man from God is the incommensurable gulf between a creator and his creatures. Nor can we find *eudaimonia* or even goodness by conforming to any plan; as W. H. Auden said in paraphrase of Jeremiah, the desires of the heart are as crooked as corkscrews, and even a full sight of the good and true would not straighten them out: "I do not understand my own actions. For I do not do what I want, but I do the very thing I hate. . . . I can will what is right, but I cannot do it" [Rom. 7:15–18].[28]

The concept of history in the Bible is not meant to provide a foundation for any metaphysics, such as a *logos* provides. If in recent times we in the West have transcendentalized history in various philosophies, notably Marxism, that is only a sign of what Lévi-Strauss would call the "overvaluation of the diachronic" consequent on our making over our biblical legacy into secular and also Hellenized forms. We see it in large and small ways; doctors today begin by "taking a history" instead of consulting the diviner to see what the *logos* decrees for this day; everywhere we are obsessed by problems of continuity and revolution. We have our synchronic structures to be sure, as we have our myths, but they pale in comparison to those of ancient societies. As Barthes' work shows, we tend to trade in our myths almost as fast as our cars in our zeal to keep up, to be abreast of the latest thing. This applies to scholarship too, with some amusing results: the worst case for a scholar is to be not wrong but out of date. Lévi-Strauss says that history plays the part of a myth for us—very true, but of what other cultural tradition could one say that? This myth leads to our distinctiveness. Hence he categorizes us as a "hot" society, overvaluing change, in contrast to "cold" societies whose *telos* is endless self-replication in the same form.[29] Though some say that this distinction, like that between oral and writing cultures, is simply another form of asserting our superiority, I believe that they overstate this case, and face an enormous burden of proof when the fashionability of this kind of remark is discounted. It is, ironically, *le dernier cri*.

The intellectual processes associated with history-writing are, like our faddisms, mythoclastic (Amos Wilder's term) because they are critical, dissolvent, and revisionist. To attempt to write history as the totalized record of "what really happened" is obviously self-defeating, since only pure tautological re-creation could achieve it; there are only interpretations, offering "the real story." The sheerest narrative is already an interpretation. In the Bible this is implicitly recognized, as is the consequence that *definitive interpretation* is a contradiction in terms. Auerbach's essay shows the way: he notes that the qualities of the biblical narratives—reticence, ellipsis, "preoccupation with the problematic"—when combined with their "tyrannical" claim to truth, enjoin on the Bible "constant interpretive change in its own contest."[30] The Deuteronomists reinterpret the old histories, the prophets and later Jesus reinterpret ethics and eschatology, and the Church reinterprets Jesus and the Old Testament too, while the rabbis turn the narratives into a *logos*. But the process by which the Bible was started on its career of endless self-reinterpretation (prefiguring sectarian controversy) began before those well-known stages. As Auerbach's analysis of style shows, a revisionist dynamic inheres in the whole project, in accord with the uncapturability of Yahweh.

NOTES

1. James Barr, "The Bible as a Document of Believing Communities," in *The Bible as a Document of the University*, ed. Hans Dieter Betz (Chico, Calif.: Scholars Press, 1981), p. 35.
2. Walker Percy, "The Delta Factor," in *The Message in the Bottle* (New York: Farrar Straus & Giroux, 1975), p. 8.
3. D. S. Carne-Ross, "Center of Resistance," in *Instaurations* (Berkeley: University of California Press, 1979), p. 4.
4. Julian Jaynes, *The Origin of Consciousness in the Breakdown of the Bicameral Mind* (Boston: Houghton Mifflin, 1976), pp. 63–64, 29–30.
5. Jacques Derrida, "Signature Event Context," *Glyph* 1 (1977), pp. 182–183.
6. Jacques Derrida, *Of Grammatology*, trans G. C. Spivak (Baltimore: The Johns Hopkins University Press, 1984), p. 50.
7. From T. S. Eliot, *Knowledge and Experience in the Philosophy of F. H. Bradley*, quoted in J. Hillis Miller, *Poets of Reality of F. H. Bradley* (New York: Atheneum, 1969), pp. 131–132.
8. René Girard, *Deceit, Desire, and the Novel*, trans Y. Freccero (Baltimore: The Johns Hopkins University Press, 1965).
9. Jaynes, pp. 36, 379, 381–385. Probably the processing of external stimuli in dreams is a similar process: the narrative of the dream seeks to include a knock at the door, to keep us asleep, and "makes up a story" to contain it.
10. Hugh Kenner, *The Pound Era* (Berkeley: University of California Press, 1971), p. 39.
11. John Dominic Crossan, *The Dark Interval* (Niles, Ill.: Argus, 1975), pp. 11 and 47.

12. Alan Durant, *Ezra Pound: Identity in Crisis* (New Jersey: Barnes and Noble, 1981), p. 69.

13. Jaynes, p. 85.

14. Carne-Ross, "The Music of a Lost Dynasty," in *Instaurations*, p. 214.

15. Reinhold Niebuhr, *The Nature and Destiny of Man* (New York: Scribner's, 1941), p. 3.

16. Eric Havelock, *Preface to Plato* (New York: Grosset & Dunlap, 1967).

17. Bruno Snell, *The Discovery of the Mind*, trans. T. G. Rosenmeyer (New York: Harper, 1960), p. 65.

18. H. W. F. Saggs, *The Encounter with the Divine in Mesopotamia and Israel* (London: Athlone, 1978), pp. 1–2.

19. Erich Auerbach, "Odysseus' Scar," in *Mimesis*, trans. W. Trask (New York: Doubleday, 1957), p. 2.

20. Robert Alter, *The Art of Biblical Narrative* (New York: Basic Books, 1981), pp. 126–129. But cf. Saul's behavior in 1 Sam. 28.

21. "Meditations on a Hobbyhorse," in *Classic Essays in English*, ed. Josephine Miles (Boston: Little, Brown, 1953), p. 411.

22. See my *Ezra Pound: the Image and the Real* (Baton Rouge: Louisiana State University Press, 1969), p. 81.

23. Claude Lévi-Strauss, "The Structural Study of Myth," in *Structural Anthropology*, trans. C. Jacobson and B. G. Schoepf (New York: Doubleday, 1967), p. 212.

24. Henri Frankfort et al., *The Intellectual Adventure of Ancient Man* (Chicago: University of Chicago Press, 1946), pp. 368–369.

25. Saggs, p. 184. For Frankfort, see *The Birth of Civilization in the Near East* (New York: Doubleday, n.d.), p. 9.

26. See also Amos 5:18–20; Jer. 7:4 and 31:29–34; Ezek. 18.

27. See Jesse Gellrich, *The Idea of the Book in the Middle Ages*, forthcoming from Cornell University Press.

28. "O who can ever gaze his fill," in *Collected Poetry of W. H. Auden* (New York: Random House), p. 225. Auden thought he was getting this from Freud, of course.

29. Claude Lévi-Strauss, *The Savage Mind* (Chicago: University of Chicago Press, 1966), pp. 254 and 233–234.

30. Auerbach, pp. 13–19.

Index

Since this is a collection of essays on and about the Bible, it would be counterproductive and needlessly verbose to include references to people or books in the Bible. Therefore, this index includes only extra-biblical scholars, writers, and works.